# KATZscan of Islam

Islam is a War.

Quran is not a peace.

ISIS is a way to Apocalypse.

By Ilya Katz
*Satirist Psychiatrist*

Published by
Katz Liberty Books.

This book is not copyrighted.
Quote it anywhere, anytime, anyplace.
Hopefully my aphorisms and cartoons
will help to win the fight
against Islamofascism

Ilya Katz, Satirist General.

ISBN 978-0-9968164-4-1

Manufactured in USA
First Print
Limited edition.

*Dear Readers,
I excavated
an ancient military manual.
No surprise
it smells quite peculiar.*

**I do not envy the rats
that meet in its path
an angry Katz!**

Truth only truth
and truth will make us free.
*Jesus Christ*

Who live by the sword,
will die by the sword.
*Jesus Christ*
*Matthew*
*26:52*

Do not be afraid of those
who kill the body but cannot kill the soul.
*Matthew*
*10:28*

Stand against the devil,
and the devil will run from you.
*James 4:7*

God did not give us a spirit that makes
us afraid, but a spirit of power
and love and self-control.
*Timothy 1:7*

Our fight is not against people
on earth but against the rulers
and authorities and the powers
of this world's darkness,
against the spiritual powers of evil
in the heavenly world.
That is why you need
to put on God's full armor.
Then on the day of evil,
you will be able
to stand strong.
And when you have finished
the whole fight,
you will still be standing.
*Ephesians 6:10*

Be strong and brave
don't be afraid of them,
and don't be frightened
because the Lord, you God,
will go with you.
*Deuteronomy 31:6*

*He who creates cartoons and aphorisms
is dedicated to fight terrorism.*

*If I will not strike with fire
if you will not strike with fire
if we will not strike with fire
who will then dispel the night?*

# FORWARD

My name is Katz. Ilya Katz.

And I am not a pussycat.

I am a descendent from King David, who did a good job on Goliath. Two thousand years ago in the main temple of Jerusalem there were letters in the worship benches – "K" and "TZ." "K" is for King, "TZ" is for high priests or Tzardeks. Only members of noble families could occupy the benches. For the next two thousand years descendants of ruling class have multiplied, and I am one of them.

My ancestors were King David, the bravest of men, and his son King Solomon who was the wisest. With such relatives I am compelled to act accordingly.

My name is Ilya, which translates from Hebrew as "strength of God."

My life was not easy, I survived the Nazi Holocaust in WWII, but lost my father and mother.

When I was born God kissed me on the forehead and blessed me with a sense of humor, but it did not coincide with the sense of humor of the Soviet rulers. To cool my temper they sent me to a Siberian hard labor concentration camp for eight years and four months.

Thirteen years ago, on September 11, I was in New York City in the Wall Street area. I had come from Miami Beach to spend a birthday with my family who live in New York. I found myself a few blocks from the World Trade Center, when the planes hit the towers. Thank God I'm still alive, but I was shocked badly by this catastrophic event. As a result of the stress, I developed diabetes (five shots of insulin every day) and uncontrollable high blood pressure. It is understandable that I have a personal account to a different types of totalitarianism, Nazism, socialism, communism and islamofascism.

I'm 80 years young now, and I dedicate my golden years to fight a personal anti-Jihad battle. I was a freedom fighter in the Soviet Union and today I have no desire to erase the war paint from my face. I am able and ready for what lies ahead of me. As my icon Ronald Reagan once said, "Don't be scared, be prepared."

The black swine flu of the Islamo-fascisim tsunami tries to influence our lives and enslave our children. We fought against Nazism, we fought against Communism, and we have no other choice but to fight against Islamofascism.

As a concerned responsible citizen, I solemnly swear that I will support and defend the Constitution of the United States against all enemies foreign and domestic.

To start my personal anti-Jihad I will present a mosaic quotations from the sacred book of Islam, Quran, and the Hadith, Book of Life and the teachings from the messenger of Allah, MuhamMAD. You will see that today no one has hijacked Islam, as has been claimed. There is no need to radicalize believers. Islam is Islam, it inherently does so. Allah and MuhamMAD are not vegetarians; they are cruel bloodsuckers.

You will read quotations from the Dark Ages and also my satirical comments. You will see that terrorists from ISIS are not a new radical breed; they are direct mainstream followers of the Quran's barbaric orders from Allah and his accomplice MuhamMAD. After 1400 years ISIS practices the same extremism, cannibalism and supremacism.

This is the core and essence of Islam. Adolf Hitler was not the originator of evil; he was a plagiarist who got the recipe for his crimes from the messenger of Allah, MuhamMAD.

The more the reader follows the steps
of the god of Islam
and the prophet of Islam,
the more he is convinced
that they are hatemongers,
spiritual fathers
of modern islamofascism.

I will abstain
from disparaging Muhammad or Allah.
I will tell the truth,
the truth is more damaging.

If one who quotes Quran and Hadith
commits blasphemy
I'm glad to boomerang against the enemy.

I report, you decide
who is wrong and who is right.

From the Dark Ages MuhumMAD inspired
the creation of khaliph@ckt vampires.

Satanic revelations
from the Prophet of Islamization.
Massacre, betrayal, and deception,
they are proven facts of MuhamMAD's perception.

My explosive aphorisms
and cartoons could backfire
but I am devoted to the land of truth and satire.

Open my book and start to read,
you will be shocked how Islam us do treat.

It is dangerous to be right
when you're fighting against a beast.
But I will not stop my satirical fight.
God will protect me with a powerful fist.

Who possess eyes will read,
who possess brains will be freed.

God did not create me to be Moses
but he did create me to be Ilya Katz.
God offered me a chance to be a hero
and I couldn't turn it down.

In a fearful time,
I try to be one of the fearless.

I don't know how to use weapons.
I am a religious man,
but nobody can stop me
from shooting satirical arrows
into indecent creatures.

This book is my attempt
to hammer an iron stake
into the rotten body
of resurrected islamofascism.

Please study my aphorisms and cartoons
in daytime
it is too scary to do so at night.

# A rat is not only animal, it's an ASSsence.

# If you dare to fight a devil maybe you are not a tiger, maybe you are just Katz!

Rats do not understand
Katz's humor;
they have different ideas
about aphorisms and cartoons.

Sometimes to make people get up
one needs to poke them
with a needle of truth.

A satirist who betrays his mission
is the same as a soldier
who left his position.

Satire is truth in life-threatening doses.

Satire's verdict is not subject to appeals.
Satire is a chemical
that dissolves fear in cannibalists-terrorists.

Satire is fine work performed with a scalpel
against a barbarian working with an axe.

Satire is the more effective tool
to counter-attack radical poison.

**It is hard
to fight with ISIS
but it is even harder
to quit living.**

God created light
the devil created darkness;
God created love
the devil created hatred;
God created Muslims
the devil created jihadists.

A black stain of islamofascisim
grows to the size
of historical disaster.

Religious totalitarianism
is the reduction of society
to the lowest common denominator.

"We can ignore reality
but we cannot ignore consequences
of ignoring reality."

*Ann Rand*

# BEWARE OF

## The antihuman extremism, radicalism, muslimofascism

*Global warming affected the brains of Presidents Bush and Obama and a flood of political correctness started..*

# President George W. Bush on Islam:

"Islam inspires countless individuals to lead lives of honesty, integrity, and morality."
*(Author's comments: How about robbery, rape and mass murder around the world in the glory of Allah and by example of the Prophet MuhamMAD?)*

"The Islam that we know is a faith devoted to the worship of one God, as revealed through The Holy Quran. It teaches the value and the importance of charity, mercy and peace…All the world continues to benefit from this faith and its achievements."
*(Author's comments: We can see it particularly in the activity of the state of Islam-ISIS).*

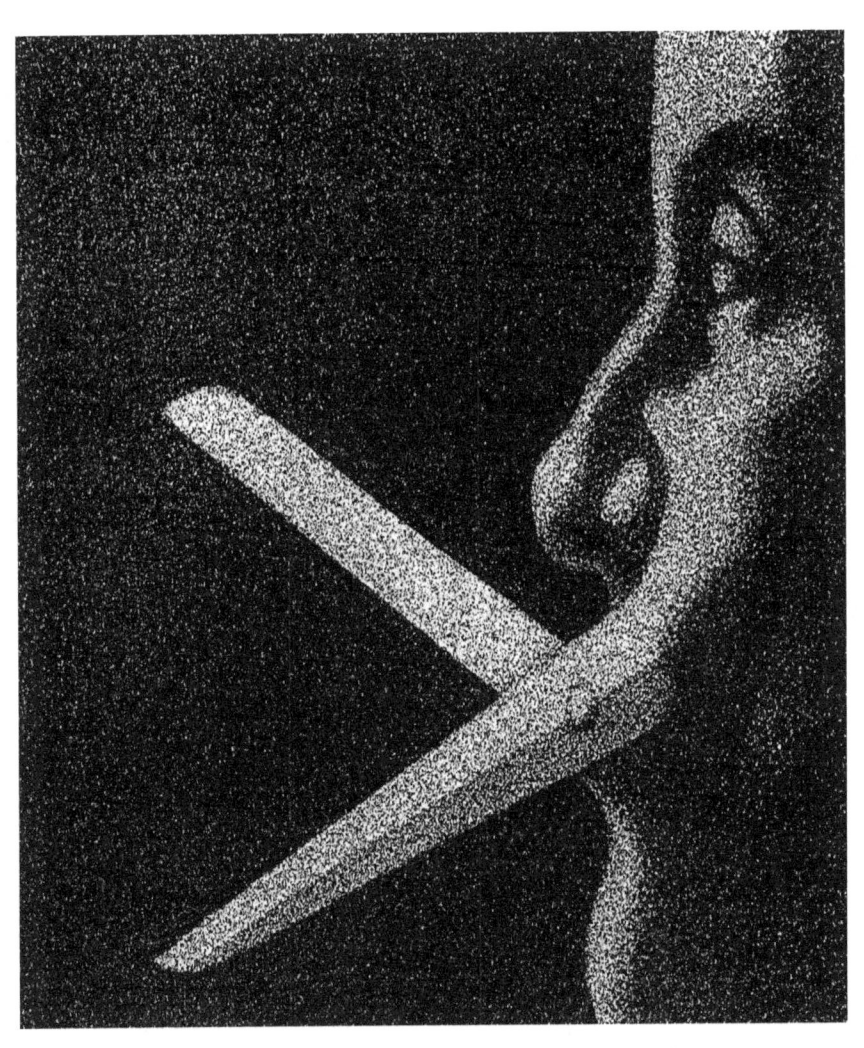

**Satirical decision:
Let's performs circumcision.**

"Americans understand we fight not a religion; ours is not a campaign against a Muslim faith. Ours is a campaign against evil."

*(Author's comments: Who commands to do evil if not the Quran and MuhamMAD? Revelations of Allah are barbaric, cannibalistic, and satanic.)*

"This new enemy seeks to destroy our freedom of expression. We value life; the terrorists ruthlessly destroy it. We value education; the terrorists do not believe women should be educated or should have health care, or should leave their homes. We value the right to speak our minds; for the terrorists, free expression can be grounds for execution. We respect people of all faiths and welcome the free practice of religion; our enemy wants to dictate how to think and how to worship even to their fellow Muslims."

*(Author's comments: Mr. President, if you have the guts to identify terrorists as muslimofascists, it would be a great speech.)*

**Politically correct ideology based on what's left from proctology.**

"I have made it clear, the war against terrorism is not a war against Muslims, nor is it a war against Arabs. It is a war against evil people who conduct crimes against innocent people."

*(Author's comments: Sure, it is not a war against a pack of wolves united with thirst for blood; it is war against the separated, non-peaceful members of the pack.")*

"The face of terror is not the true faith of Islam. That's not what Islam is all about. Islam is peace. These terrorists don't represent peace. They represent evil and war."

*(Author's comments: The sacred duty of Muslims is a permanent Jihad-war against infidels where all atrocities are not only permitted but demanded.)*

**Anyone can pretend to be an idiot. But please don't overdo it.**

# *President Barack Obama on Islam:*

"The future must not belong to those who slander the Prophet of Islam."
*(Author's comment: Why slander? The truth is more damaging.)*


"Islam demonstrated through words and deeds the possibilities of religious tolerance and racial equality."
*(Author's comments: Are you kidding, Mr. President? Are you watching the news on TV?)*


"Islam has a proud tradition of tolerance."
*(Authors comments: Please read in the Quran "Verse of the sword.")*


"No religion is responsible for terrorism; people are responsible for violence and terrorism."
*(Author's comment: Really? Islam ignites, demands, commands and rewards violence.)*

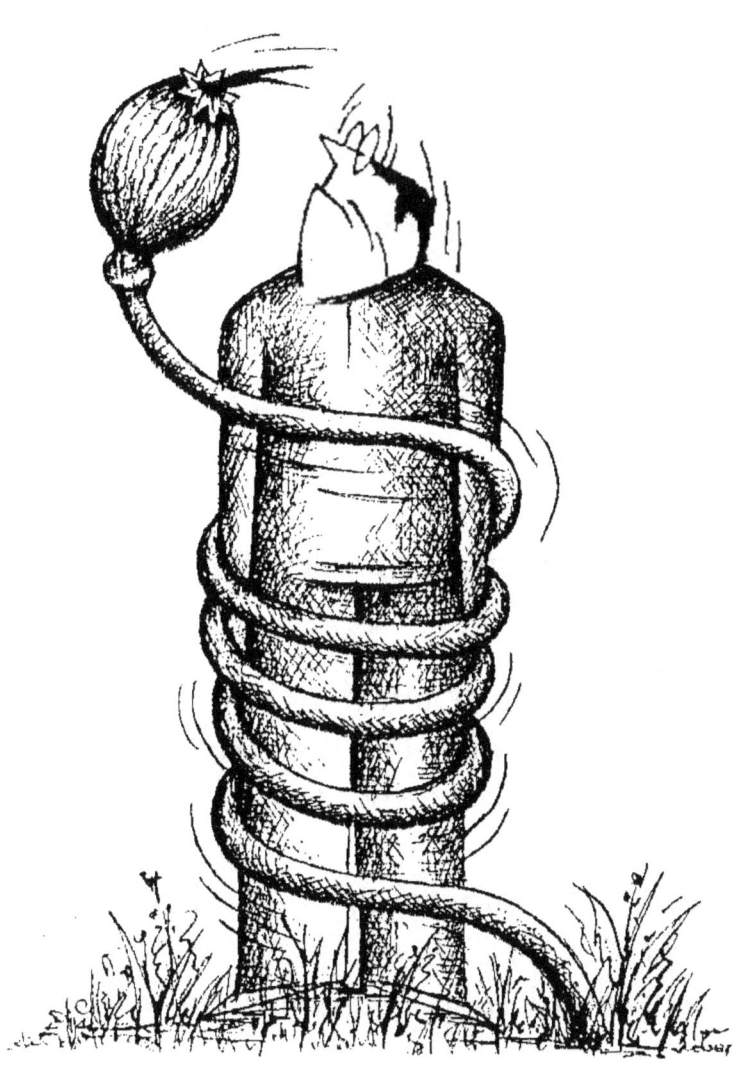

**If Islam is a religion of peace why must personal liberty be ceased?**

"Islam has been woven into the fabric of our country since its founding."
(Author's comments: Our country was built on a foundation of Judo-Christian traditions. I have no doubt that Islam is well woven into the fabric of your government, Mr. President.)

"As a student of history I also know civilization's debt to Islam."
(Author's comments: You are a lousy student. Islam brutally destroyed other civilizations.)

"You will convey our deep appreciation for the Islamic faith which has done so much over the centuries to shape the world including in my own country."
(Author's comments: Through the centuries Muslims have killed 270 million people. Mr. President, are you considering this shape of the world?")

"The sweetest sound I know is the Muslim call to Prayer."
(Authors comments: One could get diabetes from such sweets.)

"Islam has always been part of America."

*(Author's comments: I hope America will never be a part of Islam.)*


"America and Islam are not exclusive and need not be in competition. Instead they overlap and share common principles of justice and progress, tolerance and the dignity of all human beings."

*(Author's comments: If America and Islam start to share common principles I will buy a rocket and fly to God to ask for asylum.)*


"I made clear that America is not and never will be at war with Islam."

*(Author's comments: Islam is already at war with America. By the way, Mr. President, what is our military doing in Afghanistan, Iraq and Libya? I believe they are not on vacation.)*

**You have a right...
to remain silent.**

# *Quotations on the Islam situation:*

## *Guess what Bush said, what said Obama; is it not mental deficiency panorama?*

"Ours is a war not against a religion, not against the Muslim faith. But ours is a war against individuals who absolutely hate what America stands for."

"They are terrorists, and we are not at war with Islam. We are at war with people who have perverted Islam."

"The terrorists are traitors to their own faiths, trying in effect to hijack Islam itself."

**Nature does not tolerate a vacuum.
That is why
the position vacated
by the incompetent one,
is immediately occupied by another.**

"How do we, as people of faith, reconcile these realities – the profound good, the compassion and love that can flow from all of our faiths, operating alongside those who seek to hijack religion for their own murderous ends?"

"There are thousands of Muslims who proudly call themselves Americans, and they know what I know: that the Muslim faith is based upon peace and love and compassion."

"This great religion, in the hands of a few extremists, has been distorted to justify violence."
(Author's comments:
    *Distorted thinking. Think again.*
    *Why do you throw facts in vain?)*

"In God we trust," but tolerance is rust.

"Our war is not against Islam, or against faith practiced by the Muslim people. Our war is a war against evil."

*Quaranic teaching inspires attack*

"Our enemy doesn't follow the great traditions of Islam. They've hijacked a great religion."

***Too bad: real truth doesn't inform George or Barack.***

## *Our presidents unite with very special delusional faith.*

"Jihad is a holy struggle, a legitimate tenet of Islam, meaning to purify oneself or one's community."

*John O. Brennan*
*Chief of Homeland Security*

"Islam teaches tolerance, not hatred; universal brotherhood, not enmity; peace, and not violence."

*Perves Musharraf*

"Muslims are not bloodthirsty people. Islam is a religion of peace that forbids the killing of the innocent."

*Abdullah of Saudi Arabia*

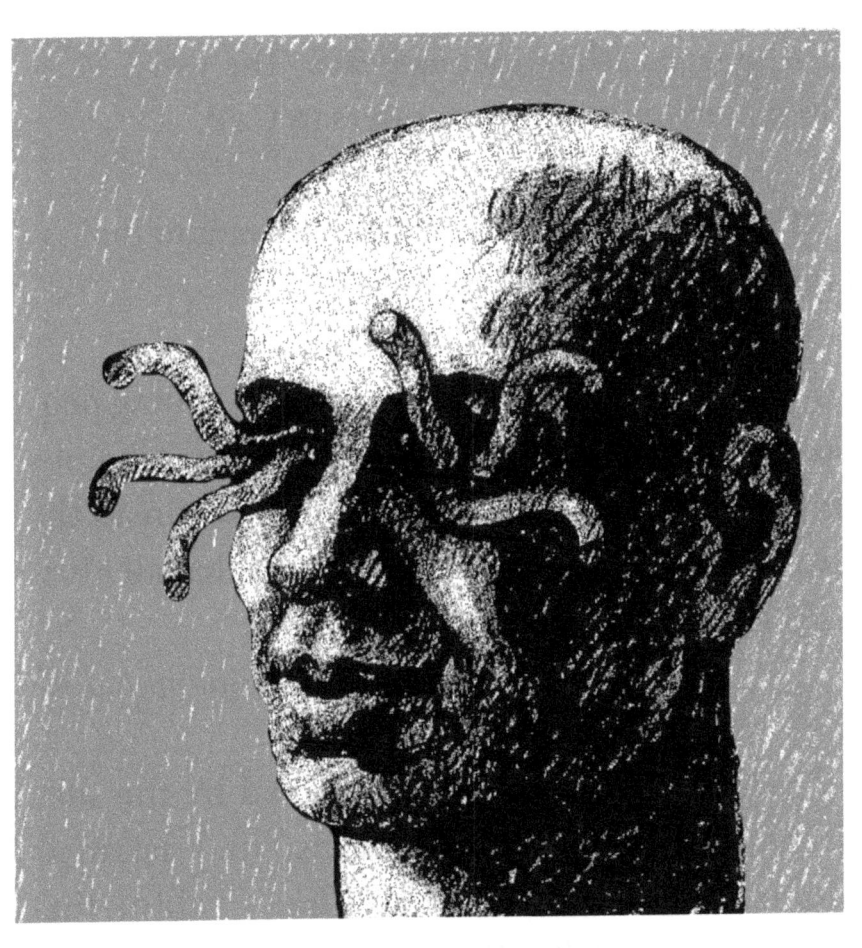

**MUSLIM EXTREMISM turns into bipolar disease, religious autism and blind dogmatism.**

"The word Islam means peace. The word Muslim means 'one who surrenders to God.'"

"I'm just hoping that people understand that Islam is peace and not violence."

"Terrorists are not following Islam. Killing people and blowing up people and dropping bombs in places and all this is not the way to spread the word of Islam. So people realize now that all Muslims are not terrorists."

*Muhammad Ali*

"I think Islam has been hijacked by the idea that all Muslims are terrorists; that Islam is about hate, about war, about jihad – I think that hijacks the spirituality and beauty that exists within Islam. I believe in allowing Islam to be seen in context and in its entirety and be judged on what it really is, not what you think it is."

*Assif Mandvi*

**Prophet who prefers the profit.**

# *Ayatollah Khomeini on Islam:*

"Those who know nothing of Islam pretend that Islam counsels against war. Those (who say this) are witless."

"People cannot be made obedient except with the sword!"

"The sword is the key to Paradise, which can be opened only for the Holy Warriors!"

"Islam says, whatever good there is, exists thanks to the sword and the shadow of the sword!"

The Ayatollah Khomeini says to the scorned, "Islam is a religion of a peace crowd; I spit upon those foolish souls who make such a claim."

(*Author's comment: Make your intelligent decision on who the real authority is on Islam: Bush and Obama, or Ayatollah Khomeini, world famous leader of Islam.*)

**ISIS follows Islamic law, but with an ass in front.**

# President John Quincy Adams on Islam:

"In the seventh century of the Christian era a wandering Arab, of the lineage of Hagar, the Egyptian, combing the powers of transcendent genius with the preternatural energy of a fanatic and the fraudulent spirit of an imposter, adopting, from the sublime conception of the Mosaic Law, the doctrine of one omnipotent God, he connected indissolubly with it the audacious falsehood, that he was himself his prophet and apostle.

He proclaimed himself as a messenger from Heaven, and spread desolation and delusion over an extensive portion of the earth... declared... exterminating war... a war of more than twelve hundred years has already raged. That war is yet flagrant; nor can it cease but by the extinctive of that imposture (Islamic religion) ...declared... exterminating war as part of his religion against all the rest of mankind."

**MuhamMAD is the first khalif.
Murderer, lier and thief.**

"The essence of his doctrine was violence and lust; the essence of his doctrine was... to exalt the brutal over the spiritual part of human nature."

"While the merciless and dissolute are encouraged to furnish motives to human action, there never can be peace on earth and good will toward men. The hand of Ishmael will be against every man, and every man's hand against him."

*(Author's comments: Thank God the disease of political correctness was not known two hundred years ago.)*

**ISIS leader is a fellow who will lay down your life for his country.**

# Winston Churchill on Islam:

"How dreadful are the curses which Mohammedanism lays on its votaries! Besides the fanatical frenzy, which is as dangerous in a man as hydrophobia in a dog, there is this fearful fatalistic apathy. The effects are apparent in many countries.

A degraded sensualism deprives this life of its grace and refinement; the next of its dignity and sanctity. The fact that in Mohammedan law every woman must belong to some man as his absolute property — either as a child, a wife, or a concubine — must delay the final extinction of slavery until the faith of Islam has ceased to be a great power among men.

Thousands become the brave and loyal soldiers of the faith: all know how to die but the influence of the religion paralyses the social development of those who follow it. No stronger retrograde force exists in the world. Far from being moribund, Mohammedanism is a militant and proselytizing faith. It has already spread throughout Central Africa, raising fearless warriors at every step; and were it not that Christianity is sheltered in the strong arms of science, the science against which it had vainly struggled, the civilisation of modern Europe might fall, as fell the civilisation of ancient Rome."

# QURAN

"Be conscious of God
and speak always the truth."

*Quran Surah 9: 119*

That is my only intention
and that is what I will do.

*Ilya Katz*

"God reveals the Book to you, and wisdom, and teaches you that which you did not know. The grace of God towards you has been very great."

*Quran 4:113*

"And remember God's grace upon you, and that which He has revealed unto you of Scripture and wisdom wherby He exhorts you."

*Quran Verse 2:231*

**ISLAMOFASCISM starts with robbery and destrution. What it will end with only God knows.**

Those who are deeply rooted in knowledge say, "We believe in it, the whole of the divine writ is from our Sustainer…"
*Quran Surah 3:7*

The only true faith in God's light is Islam. Allah accepts the repentance of whom He wills. Allah is All-Knowing, All-Wise.
*Quran Surah 9:14-15*

"The Guidance of Allah, that is the (only) Guidance. Wert thou to follow their desires after the knowledge which hath reached thee, then wouldst thou find neither Protector nor helper against Allah".
*Hadith, Al Bukhari*

He alone is God in the heavens and in the earth.
*Quran Surah 43:84*

**Americanization of the Third World was a milestone while the MUSLIMONIZATION of America will be a gravestone.**

In the name of Allah, the Beneficent, the Merciful.
Praise be to Allah, Lord of the Worlds,
The Beneficent, the Merciful.
Master of the Day of Judgment,
Thee we worship; thee we ask for help.
Show us the straight path, the path of those whom Thou hast favored; not of those who earn Thine anger nor of those who go astray.

*Quran Surah 1:1-7*

The command belongs to God alone. He commands you not to worship anyone except Him. This is the right way of life.

*Quran Surah 12:40*

Lo! Those who believe and strive in the way of Allah, these have hope of Allah's mercy. Allah is Forgiving, Merciful.

*Quran Surah 2:218*

**Orders from SHARIAH try to substitute for conscience.**

# Let's see from Hadith and Quran the roots of evil - ISIS, Taliban.

Allah is an enemy to the disbelievers.
*Quran Surah 2:98*

And Satan and his minions are their friends: "Lo! We have made the devil's protecting friends to take a course between this and that. These it is that are truly the unbelievers, and we have prepared for the unbelievers a disgraceful chastisement."
*Quran Surah 4:150-151*

Who is an enemy to Allah, and His angels and His messengers, and Gabriel and Michael! Then, lo! Allah is an enemy to the disbelievers.
*Quran Surah 2:98*

**Nothing is more dangerous than an IDIOT exploring the path of medieval religious bigotry and fanatism.**

You are commanded to fight although you dislike it. You may hate something that is good for you, and love something that is bad for you. Allah knows and you do not.
*Quran Surah 2:216*

Then your Lord spoke to His angels and said, "I will be with you. Give strength to the believers. I will send terror into the Kafirs' hearts, cut off their heads and even the tips of their fingers!"
*Quran Surah 8:12*

We have made for hell: they have hearts wherewith they understand not, eyes wherewith they see not, and ears wherewith they hear not. Indeed, they're entirely bestial: These are as the cattle – nay, but they are worse!
*Quran Surah 7:179*

Ye who believe! Choose not your fathers nor your brethren for friends if they take pleasure in disbelief rather than faith. Whoso of you taketh them for friends, such are wrong-doers.

*Quran Surah 9:23*

They would have you become Kafirs like them so you will all be the same. Therefore, do not take any of them as friends until they have abandoned their homes to fight for Allah's cause (jihad). But if they turn back, find them and kill them wherever they are.

*Quran Surah 4:89*

Believers! Do not take Kafirs as friends over fellow believers. Would you give Allah a clear reason to punish you?

*Quran Surah 4:144*

**The future is already not so great, because MUSLIM RADICALS started messing with it.**

Allah is the Protector of those who have faith: from the depths of darkness He will lead them forth into light. Of those who reject faith the patrons are the evil ones: from light they will lead them forth into depths of darkness. They will be companions of the fire, to dwell therein forever.
*Quran, Surah 2:257*

The punishment of those who wage war against Allah and His Messenger, and strive with might and main for mischief through the land is: execution, or crucifixion, or the cutting off of hands and feet from opposite sides, or exile from the land: that is their disgrace in this world, a heavy punishment is theirs in the Hereafter.
*Quran, Surah 5:33*

**ISIS doesn't even let you choose your own straight jacket.**

Your Lord inspired the angels with the message, "I will terrorize the unbelievers. Therefore smite them on their necks and every joint and incapacitate them. Strike off their heads and cut off each of their fingers and toes.

*Quran, Surah 8:12*

Fight ill disbelievers wherever you find them, take them captive, beleaguer them, and lie in wait and ambush them using every stratagem of war.

*Quran, Surah 9:5*

The infidels should not think that they can get away from us. Prepare against them whatever arms and weaponry you can muster so that you may terrorize them. They are your enemy and Allah's enemy.

*Quran, Surah 8:59*

**SHARIAH minimum law is a maximum liberty blow.**

When you clash with the unbelieving Infidels in battle, smite their necks until you overpower them, killing and wounding many of them. At length, when you have thoroughly subdued them, bind them firmly, making them captives. Thereafter either generosity or ransom them based on what benefits Islam until the war lays down its burdens. Thus are you commanded by Allah to continue carrying out Jihad against the unbelieving infidels until they submit to Islam.

*Quran, Surah 47:4*

"And bear in mind which is recited in your houses of the revelation of God and of wisdom."

*Quran 33:34*

# Pluses of SHARIAH can easily transform into grating.

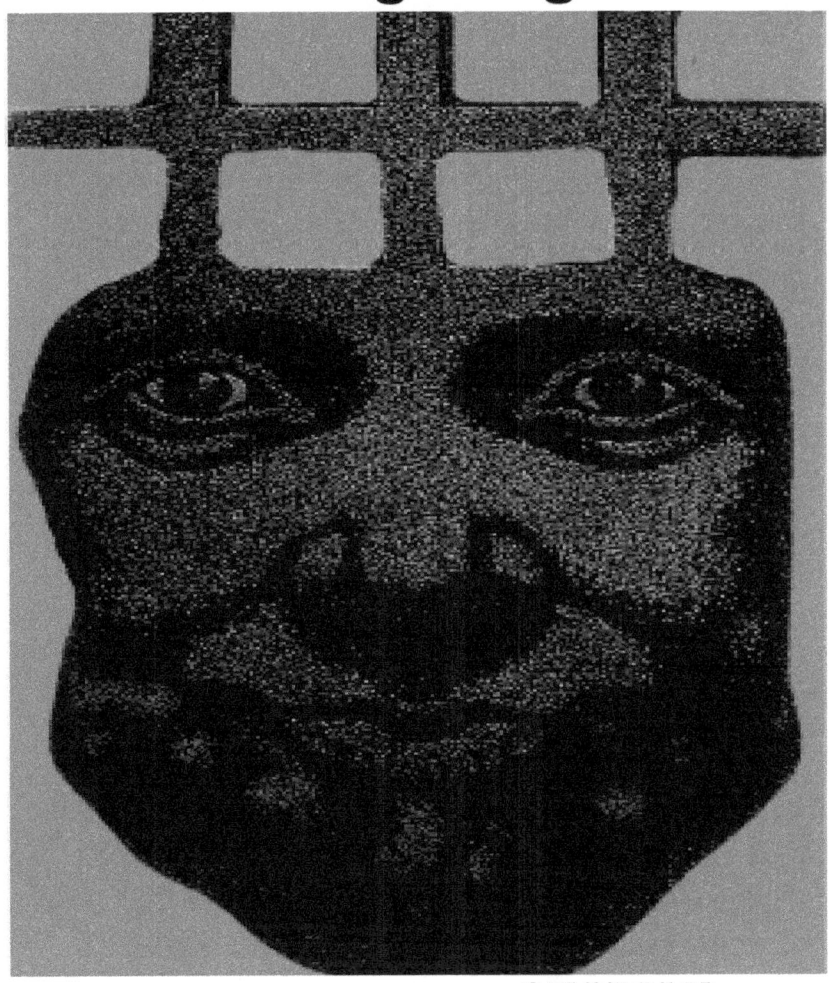

# Whatever the SHARIAH decides to build, the outcome is always the prison.

# APOSTASY

"And if any fail to judge by the light of what Allah has revealed, they are not better than those who rebel."
*Quran, Surah 5:50*

Whosoever of you turns back from his religion and dies as a disbeliever…they will be the dwellers of the Fire.
*Quran, Surah 2:217*

"Whoever changed his Islamic religion, then kill him."
*Hadith, Al Bukhari*

"Anyone who, after accepting Faith in Allah, utters Unbelief, except under compulsion, his heart remaining firm in Faith – but such as open their hear to Unbelief – on them is Wrath from Allah, and theirs will be a dreadful Penalty."
*Quran, Surah 16:106*

**A JIHADIST is a fellow who will lay down your life for his delusions.**

"Those who reject Our signs, We shall gradually visit with punishment, in ways they perceive not; respite will I grant unto them, for My scheme is strong. Allah casts terror into the hearts of the unbelievers, for that they joined companions with Allah, for which He had sent no authority. Their abode will be the Fire, and evil is the home of the wrong-doers!"

*Quran, Surah 3:151*

"As to those who reject faith, I will punish them with terrible agony in this world and in the Hereafter, nor will they have anyone to help."

*Quran, Surah 3:56*

"Now have I repented indeed; nor of those who die rejecting Faith: for them have We prepared a punishment most grievous."

*Quran, Surah 4:18*

**Allah became the first abstractionist by creating a symbiosis of a rat and hyena, it is called JIHADIST.**

"The fire whose fuel is men and stones, which is prepared for those who reject Faith."
*Quran, Surah 2:24*

"And if any fail to judge by the light of what Allah has revealed, they are no better than unbelievers."
*Quran, Surah 5:47*

To him who willingly opens up his heart to a denial of the truth: upon all such falls God's condemnation, and tremendous suffering awaits them.
*Quran, Surah 16:106*

Faith, and die rejecting, never would be accepted from any such as much gold as the earth contains, though they should offer it for ransom. For such is a penalty grievous, and they will find no helpers.
*Quran, Surah 3:90-91*

# MuhamMAD

Say (O MuhamMAD) has brought it (the Quran) down from you Lord with truth, and it may make firm and strengthen (the Faith of) those who believe, and as a guidance and glad tidings to those who have submitted (to Allah as Muslims).
*Quran, Surah 16:102*

"The (Quran) was sent down by Him who knows the mystery (that is) in the heavens and the earth: verily He is Oft-Forgiving, Most Merciful."
*Quran, Surah 25:4-6*

# Prophet of vampires.

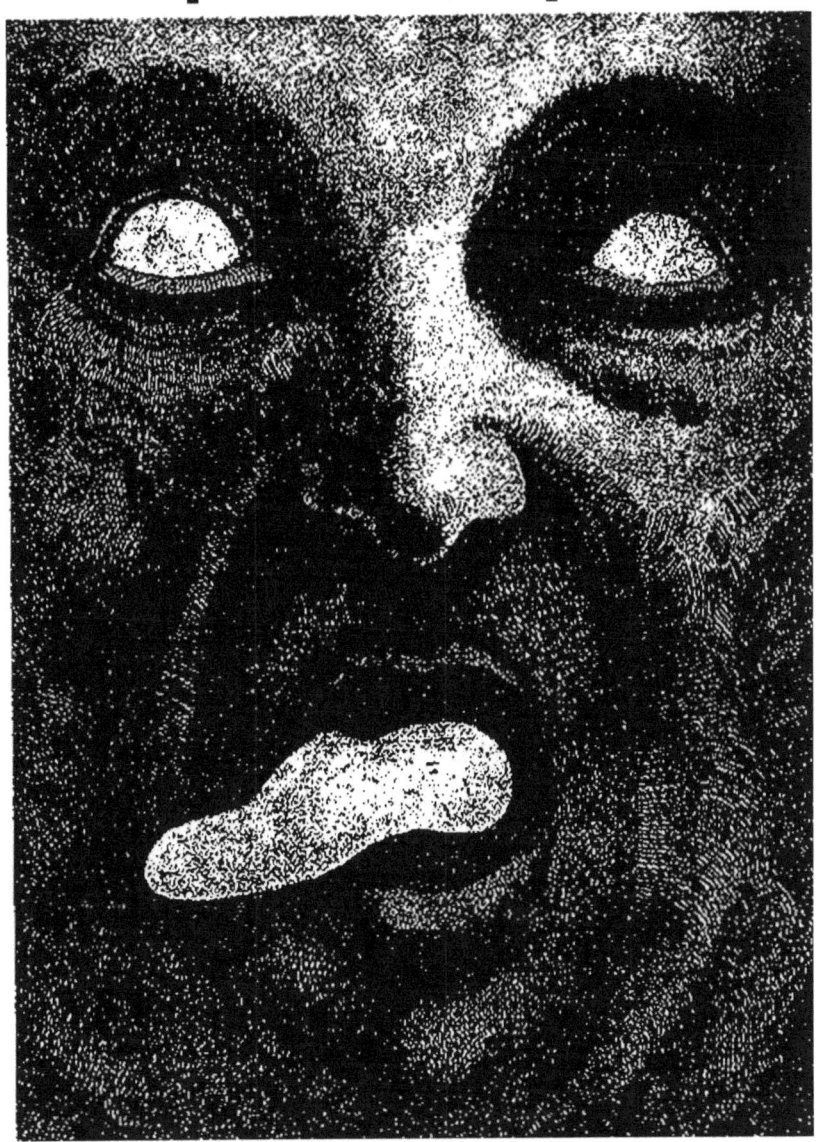

# ALLAHlination and Zombiefication will lead to elimination.

The Prophet said, "Verily, I have five names. I am MuhamMAD (Made for Praise): I am Ahmad (Most Praised); I am al-Mahi (The Effacer), by whom God effaces infidelity; I am al-Hashir (The Collector) who will collect mankind at my feet; and I am al-Aqib (The Successor)."

*Hadith, Al Bukhari*

"Believers, make war on the infidels who dwell around you. Deal firmly with them. Know that God is with the righteous."

*Quran, Surah 9:123*

"Lord…Give us victory over the unbelievers."

*Quran, Surah 2:286*

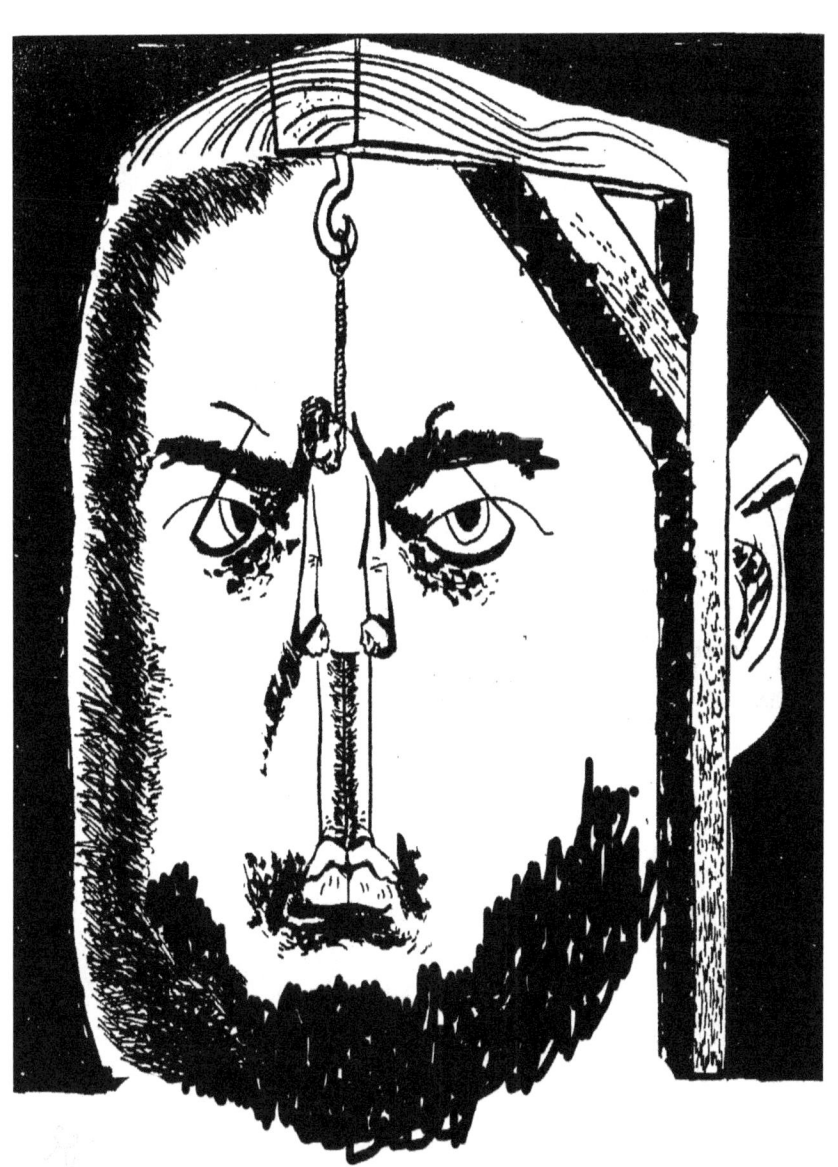

**ISLAMOFASCISM**
**is a blast from the past,
proposition of mad tradition,
sterilization of civilization.**

MuhamMAD: I have been given five things which were not given to anyone else before me:

1. Allah made me victorious by awe, by His frightening my enemies for a distance of one month's journey.

2. The earth has been made for me and for my followers, a place for praying and a place to perform rituals; therefore, anyone of my followers can pray wherever the time of prayer is due.

3. The spoils of war have been made lawful for me yet it was not lawful for anyone else before me.

4. I have been given the right of intercession on the Day of Resurrection.

5. Every Prophet used to be sent to his nation only but I have been sent to all mankind.
(Hadith, Al Bukhari 1,7,331)

**JIHADIST
has the charisma of a beast.**

The Quran calls MuhamMAD "an excellent model of conduct"
*Quran, Surah 33:21*
...and instructs Muslims: "to obey him", repeating this 21 times.

Then Allah sent His peace of reassurance down upon His messenger and upon the believers, and sent down hosts ye could not see, and punished those who disbelieved."
*Quran, Surah 9:26*

"Embrace Islam and you will be safe; embrace Islam and Allah will bestow on you a double reward. But if you reject this invitation of Islam, you shall be responsible."
*Hadith, Al Bukhari*

**Often RADICALS
are trying to heal the world,
but only with an axe
and with a sword.**

The People of the Book had faith, it were best for them: among them are some who have faith, but most of them are perverted transgressors.

*Quran, Surah 3:110*

Allah directly: "It is not fitting for a man that Allah should speak to him except by inspiration, or from behind a veil, or by the sending of a messenger to reveal, with Allah's permission, what Allah wills: for He is Most High, Most Wise."

*Quran, Surah 42:51*

"If justice is not to be found with me then where will you find it?" proclaimed MuhamMAD. But no, by your Lord, they can have no Faith, until they make you (O MuhamMAD) judge in all disputes between them, and find in themselves no resistance against your decisions, and accept (them) with full submission.

*Quran, Surah 4:65*

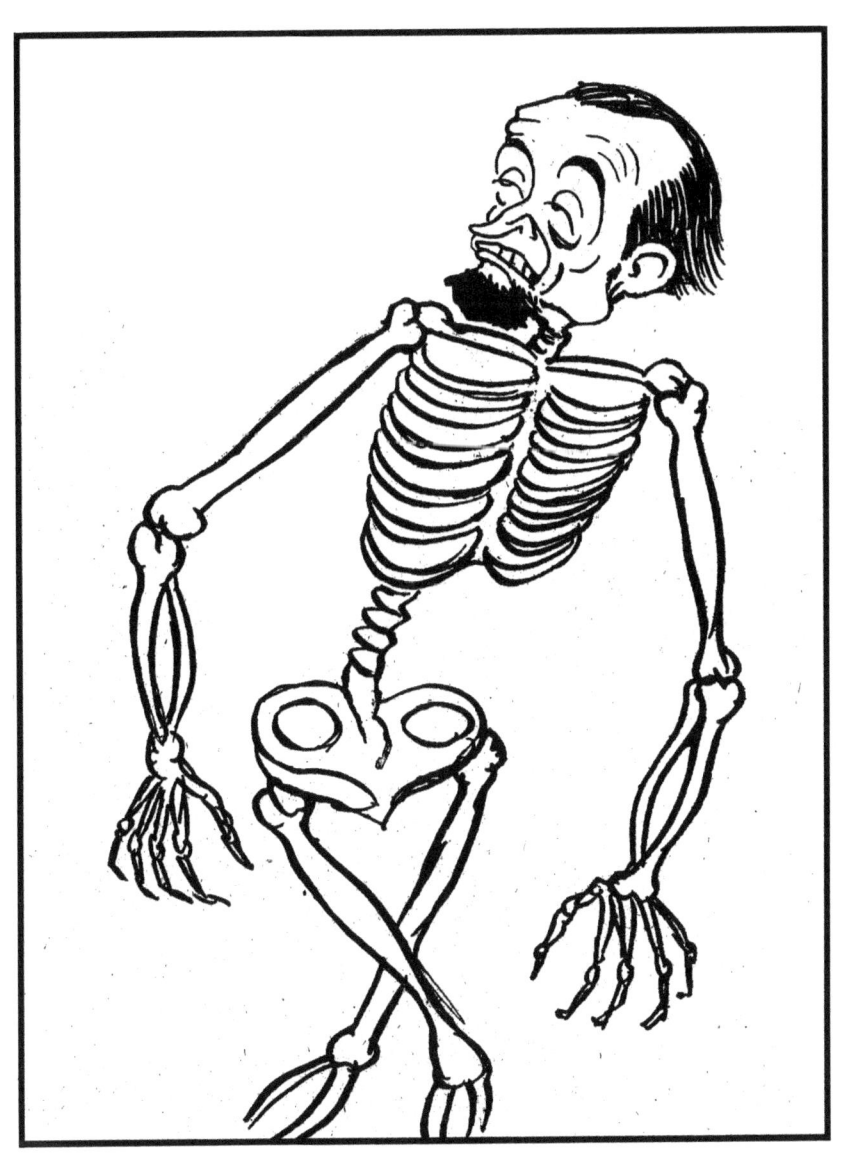

**Hundreds of years ago the skeleton MUSLIM VAMPIRE again was born.**

MuhamMAD is God's apostle. Those who follow him are ruthless to the unbelievers but merciful to one another.
*Quran, Surah 48:29*

Prophet, make war on the unbelievers and hypocrites and deal righteously with them. Hell shall be their home: an evil fate.
*Quran, Surah 9:73*

Let not the Unbelievers think that they can get the better: they will never frustrate. Against them make ready your strength to the utmost of your power, including steeds of war, to strike terror into the enemies, of Allah and your enemies, and other besides whom you may not know, but whom Allah knows.
*Quran, Surah 8:59-60*

ISIS is a genie freed by the devil.
ISIS is a torch of the darkness,
lighting the way to hell.

# JIHAD

And make ready against them all you can of power, including steeds of war to threaten the enemy of Allah...
*Quran, Surah 8:60*

So fight them until there is no more disbelief and all submit to the religion of Allah alone.
*Quran, Surah 8:39*

Those who reject Faith, and die rejecting, on them is Allah's curse, and the curse of angels, and of all mankind.
*Quran, Surah 2:161*

Verily Allah has cursed the unbelievers and prepared for them a blazing fire.
*Quran, Surah 33:64*

I shall terrorize the infidels. So wound their bodies and incapacitate them because they oppose Allah and His Apostle.
*Quran, Surah 8:12*

MuhamMAD said: "I have been commanded to fight against people; they testify that there is no god but Allah, and believe in me (that) I am the messenger (from the Lord) and in all that I have brought. And when they do it, their blood and riches are guaranteed protection on my behalf except where it is justified by law, and their affairs rest with Allah." (Hadith, Al Bukhari) The obverse is also true: if they do not become Muslims, their blood and riches are not guaranteed any protection from the Muslims.

"We hurl the truth against falsehood, and it knocks out its brain, and behold, falsehood doth perish!"
*Quran, Surah 21:18*

# KHALIF@CKT creation is a death of civilization.

## JIHADIST is making his black deedsunder direct order from Allah and for the "benefit of the people."

"MuhamMAD is the messenger of Allah, and those with him are hard against the disbelievers and merciful among themselves."
Quran, Surah 48:29

They "treat it as a falsehood that they must meet Allah"
Quran, Surah 6:31
...and "believe not in the Hereafter".
Quran, Surah16:60
...They "have bartered guidance for error"
Quran, Surah 2:16

Your strength to your utmost power, including steeds of war, to strike terror into (the hearts of) the enemies of Allah and your enemies.
Quran, Surah 8:60

Do ye prefer the life of his world to the Hereafter? But little is the comfort of this life, as compared with the Hereafter. Unless ye go forth, He will punish you with a grievous penalty, and put others in your place.
Quran, Surah 9:38-39

**It is difficult to understand MUSLIMOFASCISM with brains, but it will be quite painfull to sense it with the ass.**

"O Prophet! Strive hard against the unbelievers and the Hypocrites, and be firm against them. Their abode is Hell, an evil refuge indeed. They swear by Allah that they said nothing (evil), but indeed they uttered blasphemy, and they did it after accepting Islam..."
*Quran, Surah 9:73-74*

Fight them until there is no more (disbelief) and the worship will be for Allah alone.
*Quran, Surah 8:39*

Fight and slay the unbelievers wherever ye find them, and lie in wait for them in every stratagem of war.
*Quran, Surah 9:5*

Fight those who believe not in Allah nor the Last Day, nor hold that forbidden which hath been forbidden by Allah and His Apostle, nor acknowledge the religion of truth.
*Quran, Surah 9:29*

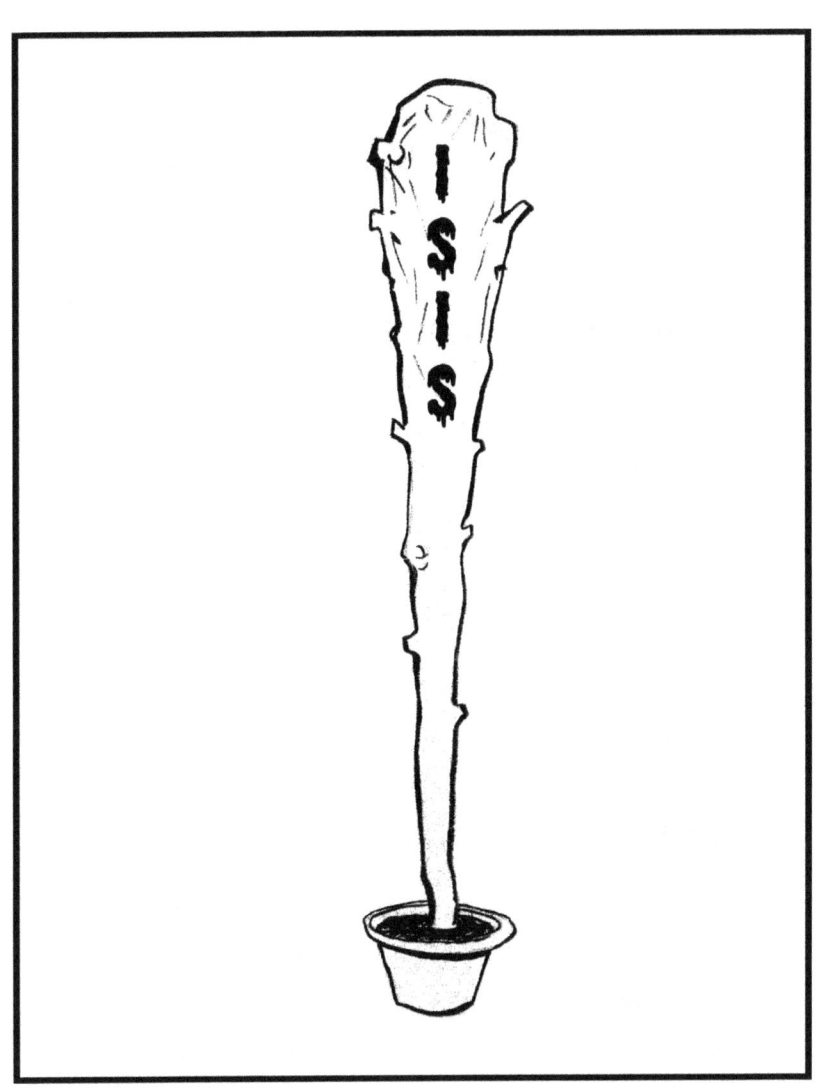

**To argue with a JIHADIST is like shaving a cactus.**

And slay them wherever ye catch them, and turn them out from where they have turned you out; for tumult and oppression are worse than slaughter; but fight them not at the Sacred Mosque, unless they (first) fight you there; but if they fight you, slay them. Such is the reward of those who suppress faith.

*Quran, Surah 2:191-193*

"This is because they contended against Allah and His Messenger. If any contend against Allah and his Messenger, Allah is strict in punishment" *(8:13)*. And the Infidels will end up in hell.

God's curse be upon the infidels! Evil is that for which they have bartered away their souls. To deny God's own revelation, grudging that He should reveal His bounty to whom He chooses from among His servants! They have incurred God's most inexorable wrath. An ignominious punishment awaits the unbelievers.

*Quran, Surah 2:89-90*

## "AL QAEDA on the run" proclaimed Obama. Too bad they're running in our direction.

Those that deny Our revelations We will burn in fire. No sooner will their skins be consumed than We shall give them other skins, so that they may truly taste the scourge. God is mighty and wise.
*Quran, Surah 4:56*

Let not the unbelievers think that they will ever get away. They have not the power to do so. Muster against them all the men and cavalry at your command, so that you may strike terror into the enemy of God and your enemy....
*Quran, Surah 8:59-60*

Those that make war against God and His apostle and spread disorder in the land shall be slain and crucified or have their hand and feet cut off on alternate sides, or be banished from the land.
*Quran, Surah 5:33*

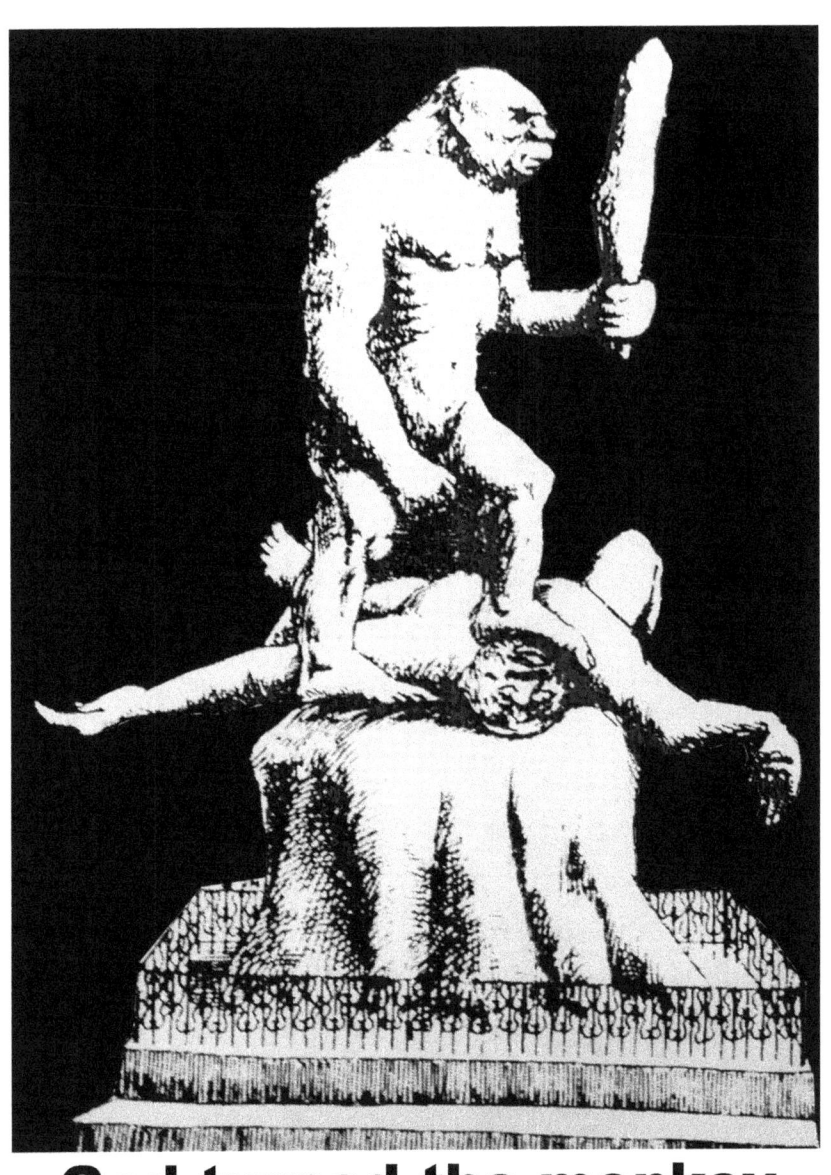

**God turned the monkey into a human being, then the devil degraded it to a JIHADIST.**

Garments of fire have been prepared for the unbelievers. Scalding water shall be poured upon their heads, melting their skins and that which is in their bellies. They shall be lashed with rods of iron. Whenever, in their anguish, they try to escape from Hell, back they shall be dragged; taste the torment of the Conflagration!

*Quran, Surah 22:19-20*

"O ye who believe! When ye meet the Unbelievers in hostile array, never turn your backs to them. If any do turn his back to them on such a day – unless it be in a stratagem of war, or to retreat to a troop (of his own) – he draws on himself the wrath of Allah, and his abode is Hell, an evil refuge (indeed)!

*Quran, Surah 8:15-16*

**Devoted JIHADIST will be surprised, instead of 70 virgins Lady Death will be his prize.**

There will no longer be two religions existing in Arabia. I descended by Allah with the sword in my hand, and my wealth will come from the shadow of my sword. And the one who will disagree with me will be humiliated and persecuted.

*Hadith, Al Bukhari*

Fighting is prescribed for you, and ye dislike it. But it is possible that ye dislike a thing which is good for you, and that ye love a thing which is bad for you. But Allah knoweth, and ye know not.

*Quran, Surah 2:216*

**TERRORIST, if you get bored in hell, I recommend you read my books.**

# WAR IS DECEIT.

Said MuhamMAD: "war is deceit. God leads whoever he wills astray."
*Quran, Surah 13:57*

"Allah has already sanctioned for you the dissolution of your vows."
*Hadith, Al Bukhari*

The Prophet said, "If I take an oath and later find something else better than that, then I do what is better and expiate my oath."
*Hadith, Al Bukhari 7:67:427*

MuhamMAD: "All lying is a sin except the one benefiting the Muslim or the one keeping him out of harm's way."
*Hadith, Al Bukhari*

**ISLAMOFASCISM shows the path to happiness. But for sure we are not going survive it.**

"If I make a pledge and later discover a more worthy pledge, then I will take the better action and make amends for my earlier promise."

*Hadith, Al Bukhari*

MuhamMAD's close follower said, "Let us smile to the face of some people (non-Muslims) while our hearts curse them. Let not the believers take the disbelievers as friends instead of the believers, and whoever does that, will never be helped by Allah in any way, unless you indeed fear a danger from them. And Allah warns you against Himself, and to Allah is the final return."

*Quran, Surah 3:28*

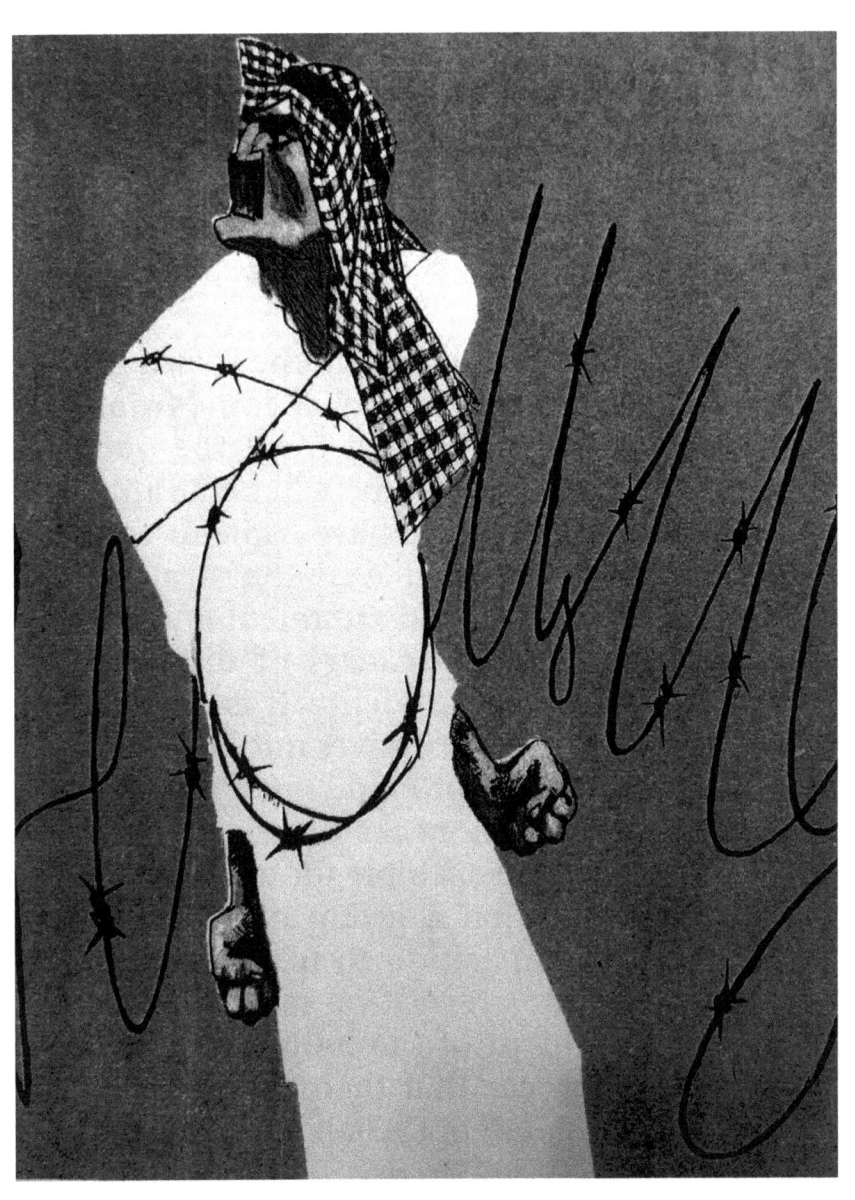

**ISIS organization is a liberty annihilation.**

# CRUELTY

I descended by Allah with the sword in my hand, and my wealth will come from the shadow of my sword. And the one who will disagree with me will be humiliated and persecuted. I have come to you as a slaughterer. He paved the straight way which contains no argument and no wheedling with the leaders of disbelief and the patrons of infidelity. It is not for any prophet to have captives until he hath made slaughter in the land…merciful, ordered to strike the necks of prisoners… and he set a good example for us.

…a mosque that a group of Muslims had built in opposition to his authority. Allah gave him a revelation making clear the malign intent of the builders: "They will indeed swear that their intention is nothing but good; but Allah doth declare that they are certainly liars.

*Quran(9:107)*

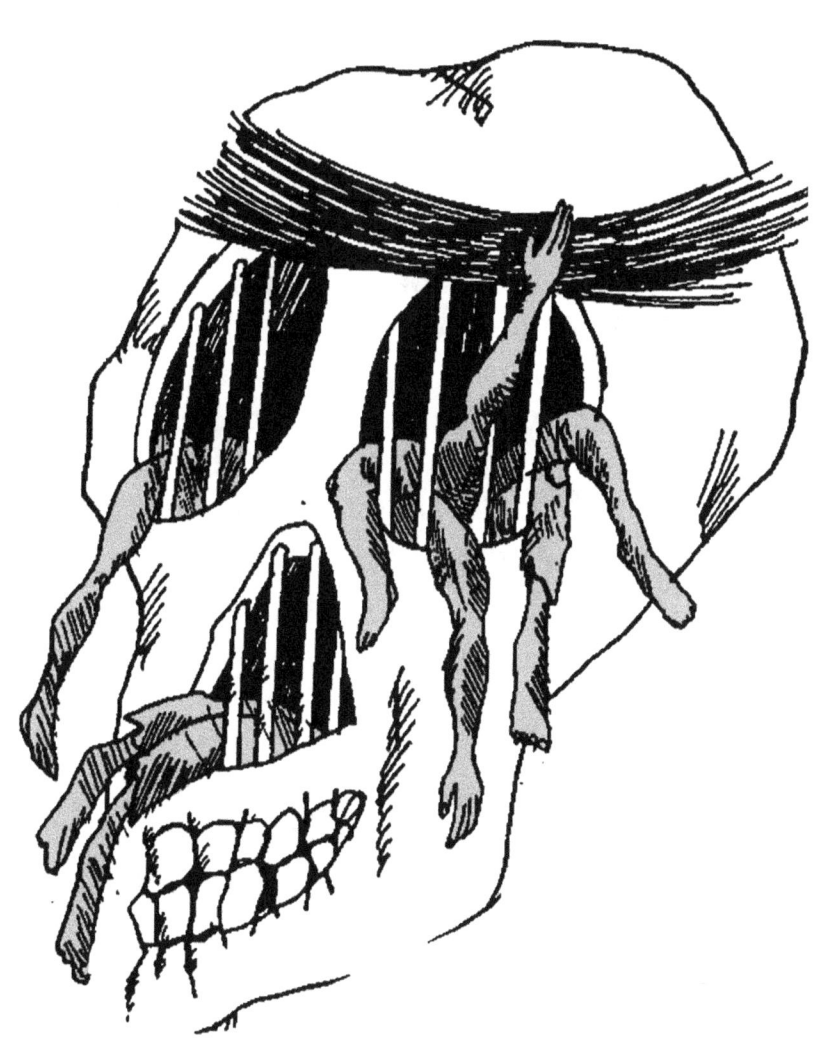

**What do the DEVIL and TERRORIST have in common? They are not human.**

Allah himself gave MuhamMAD his response to Abu Lahab in a new revelation: "May the hands of Abu Lahab perish! May he himself perish! Nothing shall his wealth and gains avail him. He shall be burnt in a flaming fire, and his wife, laden with faggots, shall have a rope of fibre around her neck!"

*Quran, Surah 111:1-5*

Those who cause corruption be punished by the amputation of their hands and feet and their eyes put out with heated iron bars, and that they be left in the desert to die. Their pleas for water, he ordered, must be refused. As to the thief, male or female, cut off his or her hands: a punishment by way of example, from Allah, for their crime; and Allah is exalted in power.

*Quran, Surah 5:38*

**Banner at the entrance to Muslim Hell reads: "Welcome to heaven."**

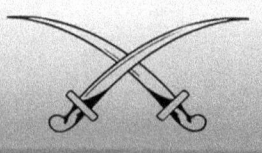

# JEWS

O you who have been given the Scripture (Jews and Christians)! Believe in what We have revealed (to Muhammad) confirming what is with you, before We efface faces (by making them like the back of necks; without nose, mouth, eyes) and turn them hindwards. And the commandment of Allah is always executed.
*Quran, Surah 4:47*

O you who believe! If you obey a party from among those who have been given the Book, they will turn you back as unbelievers after you have believed.
*Quran, Surah 3:100*

"And you will most certainly find them (the Jews) the greediest of men for life."
*Quran, Surah 2:96*

## Familiar Tongue

**JIHADIST-EXTREMIST sold his conscience to the beast.**

"And the Jews will not be pleased with you, nor the Christians until you follow their religion. Say: Surely Allah's guidance, that is the guidance. And if you follow their desires after the knowledge that has come to you, you shall have no guardian from Allah, nor any helper."
*Quran, Surah 2:120*

Allah commands, "O ye who believe! Take not the Jews and the Christians for your friends and protectors: they are but friends and protectors to each other. And he amongst you that turns to them (for friendship) is of them. Verily Allah guideth not a people unjust."
*Quran, Surah 5:51*

The Jews "strive to do mischief on earth. Allah has cursed them for their disbelief, so they believe not except a few."
*Quran, Surah 4:46*

Allah would strike "terror" into the Jews' hearts: "Of a truth ye are stronger because of the terror in their hearts by Allah."
*Quran, Surah 59:11-17*

They will be gathered unto Hell which will look like a mirage whose different side will be destroying each other. Then they will fall into the Fire. "And thou wilt find them greediest of mankind for life and (greedier) than the idolaters."
*Quran, Surah 2:96*

The Jews were covered with humiliation and misery; they drew on themselves the wrath of Allah. This is because they went on rejecting the Signs of Allah and slaying His Messengers without just cause. This because they rebelled and went on transgressing.
*Quran, Surah 2:61*

They will pay the penalty for their disobedience, arrogance, and obstinacy in this world as well as in the next.
*Quran, Surah 3:56*

Many of the People of the Scripture long to make you disbelievers after your belief, through envy on their own account, after the truth hath become manifest unto them.
*Quran, Surah 2:109*

If a lucky chance befalls you, it is evil unto them, and if disaster strikes you they rejoice thereafter. Is it ever so that when ye make a covenant a party of you set it aside? The truth is, most of them believe not."
*Quran, Surah 2:100*

"If only the People of the Book had faith, it were best for them: among them are some who have faith, but most of them are perverted transgressors"
*Quran, Surah 3:110*

**JIHADISTS have
the eyes of a raven
the ears of a donkey
and the wolf's appetite
for blood.**

Shame is pitched over them wherever they are found. They draw on themselves wrath from Allah, and pitched over them is (the tent of) destitution. This because they rejected the Signs of Allah, and slew the prophets in defiance of right: this because they rebelled and transgressed beyond bounds.

*Quran, Surah 62:5*

MuhamMAD said: "Say Amen when the Imam guides you along the right path and says, 'not the path of the Jew who deserves your anger, nor the way of the Christians who have gone astray.' All of a Muslim's past sins are forgiven when they say Amen in concert with the angels."

*Hadith, Al Bukhari B1, 12, 749*

# ISIS is Halloween upside-down.
# Animals are dressed like people.

# TERRORISTS grow like mushrooms but mostly poisonous.

MuhamMAD said: "According to Allah, any Jew or Christian that is aware of me, but dies before accepting my prophecy, will be sent to Hell."
*Hadith, M001, 0284*

MuhamMAD said: "If it weren't for the Jews, meat would not rot. If not for Eve, wives would never disobey their mates."
*Hadith, Al Bukhari B4, 55, 547*

MuhamMAD said: "May Allah curse the Jews! Allah ordered them to not eat animal fat, so what do they do? The melt it down, sell it, and invest the proceeds."
*Hadith, Al Bukhari B6, 60, 157*

MuhamMAD proclaimed, "There will never be two religions in Arabia."

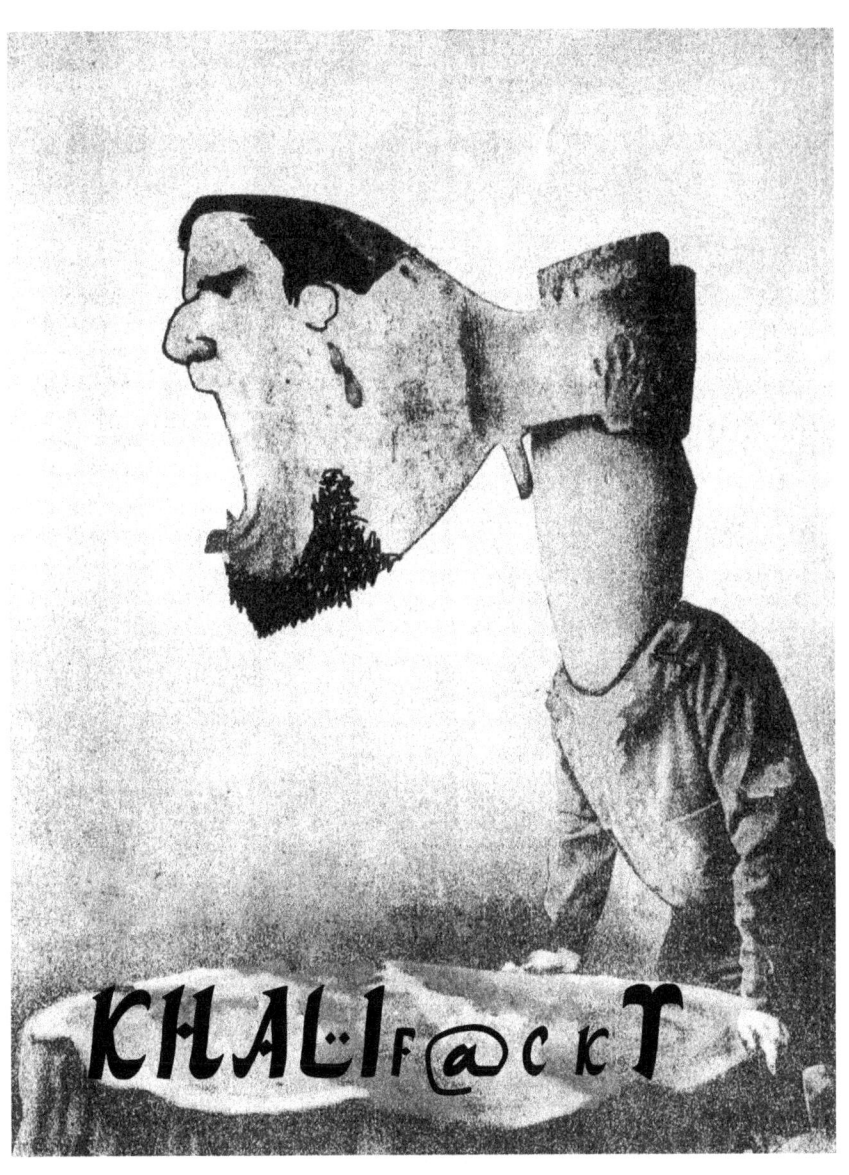

**ISIS cares about people as an axe cares about someone whom it cuts the head.**

The likeness of those who were entrusted with Taurat…but who subsequently failed in those (obligations) is as the likeness of a donkey which carries huge burdens of books. Shall I point out to you something much worse than this, by the treatment it received from Allah? Those who incurred the curse of Allah and His wrath, those of whom some He transformed into apes and swine, those who worshipped evil…

*Quran, Surah 5:60*

Be as apes, despised and hated.

*Quran, Surah 2:65*

Jews are compared to monkeys and pigs. A group of Israelites were lost. Nobody knows what they did. But I do not see them except that they were cursed and transformed into mice or rats.

*Hadith, Al Bukhari*

**The JIHADIST in his childhood dreamt to become an assassin. The dream came true.**

"You brothers of monkeys, has God disgraced you and brought His vengeance upon you?"
*Quran, Surah 2:62-65, 5:59-60, 7:166*

"Allah transformed the Sabbath-breaking Jews into pigs and monkeys. Fight those who believe not in Allah nor the Last Day, nor hold that forbidden which has been forbidden by Allah. As often as they light a fire for war, Allah extinguishes it. Their effort is for corruption in the land, and Allah loveth not corruptors."
*Quran, Surah 5:64*

"Slay the idolaters where you find them…"
*Quran, Surah 9:5*

Prophet MuhamMAD said: "I have brought slaughter upon you. They will be killed or crucified, or have their hands and feet on alternate sides cut off, or will be expelled out of the land."
*Quran, Surah 5*

Muhammad went to Medina's marketplace and told his people to dig trenches. He made all the Jewish men to go into trenches. More than eight hundred men were beheaded. Muhammad himself struck the head of some captives. Women and children were enslaved.

"Some ye slew, and ye made captive some. And He caused you to inherit their land and their houses and their wealth and land ye have not trodden…"
Quran, Surah 33:26-27

Muhammad said, "You judged them with the judgment of Allah."

Muhammad issued an order: "Kill any Jew that falls into your power." Allah's Apostle said, "The Hour will not be established until you fight with the Jews, and the stone behind which a Jew will be hiding will say, "O Muslim! There is a Jew hiding behind me, so kill him." Slay the idolaters wherever ye find them and take them, and besiege them, and prepare for them each ambush."
Quran, Surah 9:5

# KHALIF@CKT is the country of organized slavery.

## ISLAM can build only a prison. And it is a life sentence.

# WOMEN

Allah has made men superior to women because men spend their wealth to support them. Therefore, virtuous women are obedient, and they are to guard their unseen parts as Allah has guarded them. As for those women whom ye fear rebellion, admonish them and banish them to beds apart, and scourge them.
*Quran, Surah 4:34*

O Prophet! Tell your wives and your daughters and the women of the believers to draw their cloaks all over their bodies…That will be better, that they should be known so as not to be annoyed.
*Quran, Surah 33:59*

**Isn't it time to rise and fight MUSLIMOFASCIST genocide?**

And say to the believing women that they cast down their looks and guard their private parts and do not display their ornaments except what appears thereof, and let them wear their head-coverings over their bosoms, and not display their ornaments except to their husbands or their fathers, or the fathers of their husbands, or their sons, or the sons of their husbands, or their brothers, or their brothers' sons, or their sisters' sons, or their women, or those whom their right hands possess, or the male servants not having need (of women), or the children who have not attained knowledge of what is hidden of women; and let them not strike their feet so that what they hide of their ornaments may be known; and turn to Allah all of you, O believers! so that you may be successful."

*Quran, Surah 24:31*

## What is the reason to suffer in prison?

And stay in your houses, and do not display yourselves like that of the times of ignorance.

*Quran, Surah 33:33*

"Allah permits you to shut them in separate rooms and to beat them, but not severely. If they abstain, they have the right to food and clothing. Treat women well for they are like domestic animals and they possess nothing themselves. Allah has made the enjoyment of their bodies lawful in his Quran."

*Hadith, Al Bukhari*

Your women are a tilth for you so go to your tilth as ye will.

*Quran, Surah 2:223*

Mohammad said: A man will not be asked as to why he beat his wife.

**If America will dig too deep into the history, it might exhume a skeleton of discrimination.**

Mohammed asked, "Is not the value of a woman's eye-witness testimony half that of a man's? That is because a woman's mind is deficient.
*Hadith, Al Bukhari 3,48,826*

Marry women of your choice, two or three or four; but if ye fear that ye shall not be able to deal justly (with them), then only one, or (a captive) that your right hands possess, that will be more suitable, to prevent you from doing injustice.
*Quran, Surah 4:3*

Allah directs you as regards your children: to the male, a portion equal to that of two females.
*Quran, Surah 4:11*

If there are brethren, men and women, then the male shall have the like of the portion of two females.
*Quran, Surah 4:176*

**Reduction of humanism to cannibalism, it is exactly MUSLIMOFASCISM.**

Get two witnesses, out of your own men, and if there are not two men, then a man and two women, such as ye choose, for witnesses, so that if one of them errs, the other can remind her.
*Quran, Surah 2:282*

Mohammed said, "confront this man's wife and if she admits committing adultery have her stoned to death."
*Hadith, Al Bukhari 3,38,508*

Ali had a woman stoned to death on a Friday and said, "I have punished her as Mohammed would have. Lo! I confirm that the penalty of Rjam be inflicted on him who commits illegal sexual intercourse, if he is already married and the crime is proved by witnesses or pregnancy or confession…surely Allah's messenger carried out the penalty of Rajam, and so did we after him."
*Hadith, Al Bukhari 8,82,803*

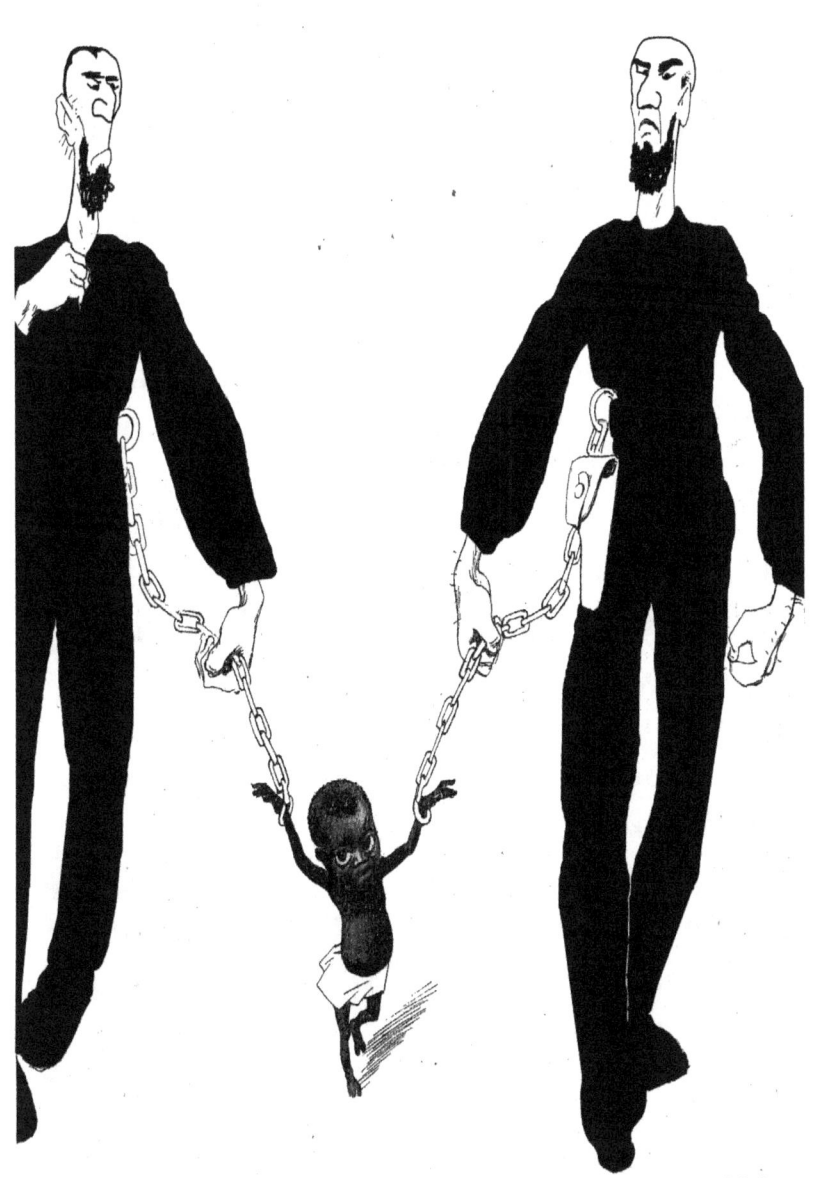

A woman came to the Messenger of Allah, may Allah bless him and grant him peace, and informed him that she had committed adultery and was pregnant. The Messenger of Allah, may Allah bless him and grant him peace, said to her, "Go away until you give birth." When she had given birth, she came to him. The Messenger of Allah, may Allah bless him and grant him peace, said to her, "Go away until you have suckled and weaned the baby." When she had weaned the baby, she came to him. "He said, "Go and entrust the baby to someone." She entrusted the baby to someone and then came to him. He gave the order and she was stoned.

*Hadith, Al Bukhari*

**A monkey was turned into a human, then into a RADICAL and by doing so, it was turned back into an animal.**

"O women! Give alms, as I have seen that the majority of the dwellers of hellfire were you. You curse frequently and are ungrateful to your husbands. I have not seen anyone more deficient in intelligence and religion than you. A cautious sensible man could be led astray by some of you."

"A nation who will put a woman in a high position will never succeed. A man is superior above woman, and a man should be in a position like this, not a woman."

*Quran, Surah 4*

**MUSLIMOFASCIST'S wind most often blows from the direction of where the legs grow.**

# REWARD FOR FIGHT FOR ALLAH

On the Day of Resurrection, a call-maker will announce, "Let every nation follow that which they used to worship." Then none of those who used to worship anything other than Allah like idols and other deities but will fall in Hell, till there will remain none but those who used to worship Allah, both those who were obedient…
*Hadith, Al Bukhari*

And if ye are slain, or die, in the way of Allah, forgiveness and mercy from Allah are far better than all they could amass. And if ye die, or are slain, lo! It is unto Allah that ye are brought together.
*Quran, Surah 3:157-58*

# Jihadist's brain evolution.

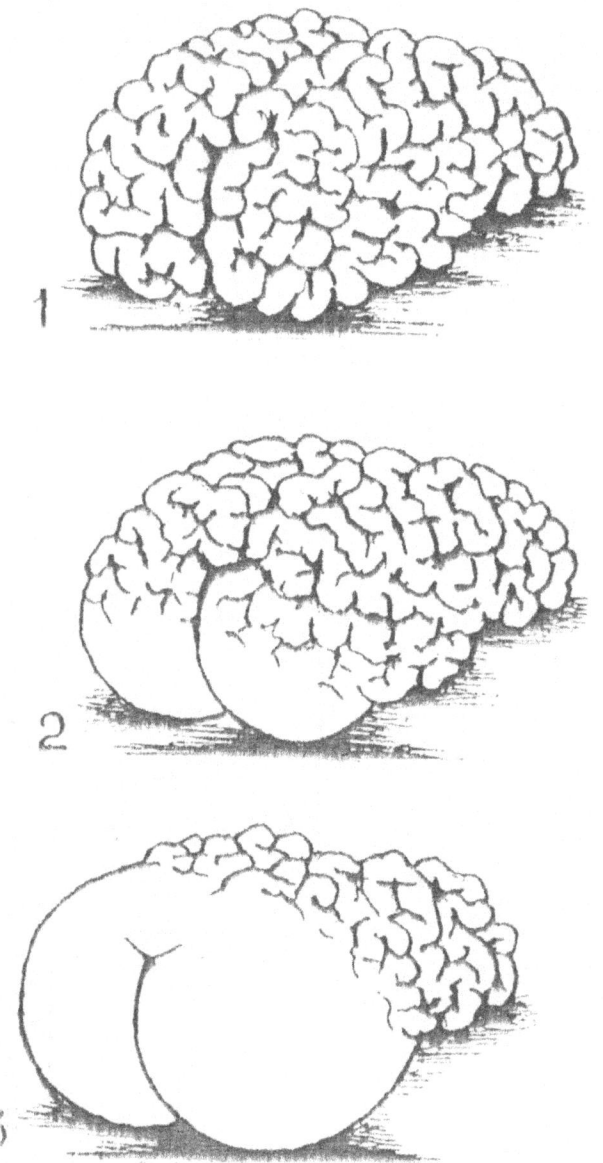

# Free fall can create only a dummy asshole.

He who forsakes his home in the cause of Allah, finds in the earth many a refuge, wide and spacious: should he die as a refugee from home for Allah and His Messenger, His reward becomes due and sure with Allah: and Allah is Oft-forgiving, Most Merciful.

*Quran, Surah 4:100*

Go forth in Allah's way, you should incline heavily to earth; are you contented with this world's life instead of the hereafter? But the provision of this world's life compared with the hereafter is but little. If you do not go forth, He will chastise you with a painful chastisement and bring in your place a people other than you, and you will do Him no harm; and Allah has power over all things.

*Quran, Surah 9:38-39*

# An aphorism is created when God kisses the author.

# Who kissed the JIHADISTS when they expected that 70 virgins will kiss them in Heaven?

Not equal are those believers who sit (at home) and receive no hurt, and those who strive and fight in the cause of Allah with their goods and their persons. Allah hath granted a grade higher to those who strive and fight with their goods and persons than to those who sit (at home). Unto all (in Faith) hath Allah promised good: but those who strive and fight hath He distinguished above those who sit (at home) by a special reward.

*Quran, Surah 4:95*

Those of the believers who sit still…are not on an equality with those who strive in the way of Allah with their wealth and lives. Allah hath conferred on those who strive with their wealth and lives a rank above the sedentary. Unto each Allah hath promised good, but He hath bestowed on those who strive a great reward above the sedentary.

*Quran, Surah 4:95*

O you who believe! Shall I guide you to ta trade that will save you from a painful torment? That you believe in Allah and His Messenger and that you strive hard and fight in the Cause of Allah with you wealth and your lives, that will be better for you, if you but know! He will forgive you your sins, and admit you into Gardens under which rivers flow, and pleasant dwellings in 'Adn Paradise; that is indeed the great success. and also another which you love, help from Allah and a near victory.

*Quran, Surah 61:10-13*

No blame is there on the blind, nor is there blame on the lame, nor on one ill: but he that obeys Allah and His Messenger will admit him to Gardens beneath which rivers flow; and he who turns back will punish him with a grievous Penalty.

*Quran, Surah 48:17*

**EXTREMISTS are divided into the sick and under-examined.**

Let those who sell the life or this world for the Hereafter fight in the Cause of Allah, and whoso fights in the Cause of Allah, and is killed or gets victory, We shall bestow on him a great reward.

*Quran, Surah 4:74*

MuhamMAD said: "Be aware that Paradise lies under the shadow of swords."

Against them make ready your strength to the utmost of your power, including steeds of war, to strike terror into (the hearts of) the enemies, of Allah and your enemies, and others besides, whom ye may not know, but whom Allah doth know. Whatever ye shall spend in the cause of Allah, shall be repaid unto you, and ye shall not be treated unjustly.

*Quran, Surah 8:60*

**A slave could be brave. But the brave will not agree to be a slave.**

But those who are slain in the way of Allah, He will never let their deeds be lost.
*Quran, Surah 47:4*

Allah will put this dust on the face of your killer, and he will kill your killer. Allah assigns for a person who participates in (holy battles) in Allah's Cause and nothing causes him to do so except belief in Allah and His Messengers, that he will be recompensed by Allah either with a reward, or booty (if he survives) or will be admitted to Paradise (if he is killed in the battle as a martyr).
*Hadith, Al Bukhari*

Allah has preferred in grades those who strive hard and fight with their wealth and their lives above those who sit (at home). Unto each, Allah has promised good (Paradise), but Allah has preferred those who strive hard and fight above those who sit (at home) by a huge reward.
*Quran, Surah 4:95*

**A JIHADIST'S actions are guided by only his wrinkle; the one he sits on.**

MuhaMAD said: "The rest of the year is Haji. Even jihad is inferior unless a man knowingly risks and loses both life and property for the sake of Allah."
*Hadith, Al Bukhari*

"The man who fights to make Islam dominant is the man who fights for Allah's cause."
*Hadith, Al Bukhari*

"Anyone who even gets his feet dirty performing jihad will be saved from Hell by Allah."
*Hadith, Al Bukhari*

Spend your wealth generously for Allah's cause (jihad) and do not use your own hands to contribute to your destruction. Do good, for surely Allah loves those that do good."
*Hadith, Al Bukhari*

**ISIS is like a field
of poisonous weeds,
unspeakable deeds
ignoring human pleads.**

Think not of those who are killed in the way of Allah as dead. Nay, they are alive, with their Lord, and they have provision. They rejoice in what Allah has bestowed upon them of His Bounty, rejoicing for the sake of those who have not yet joined them, but are left behind (not yet martyred) that on them no fear shall come, nor shall they grieve. They rejoice in a Grace and a Bounty from Allah, and that Allah will not waste the reward of the believers.

*Quran, Surah 3:169-171*

And amongst them will be passed round vessels of silver and cups of crystal…and round about them will boys of everlasting youth. If you see them, you would think them scattered pearls.

*Quran, Surah 76:5, 15, 19*

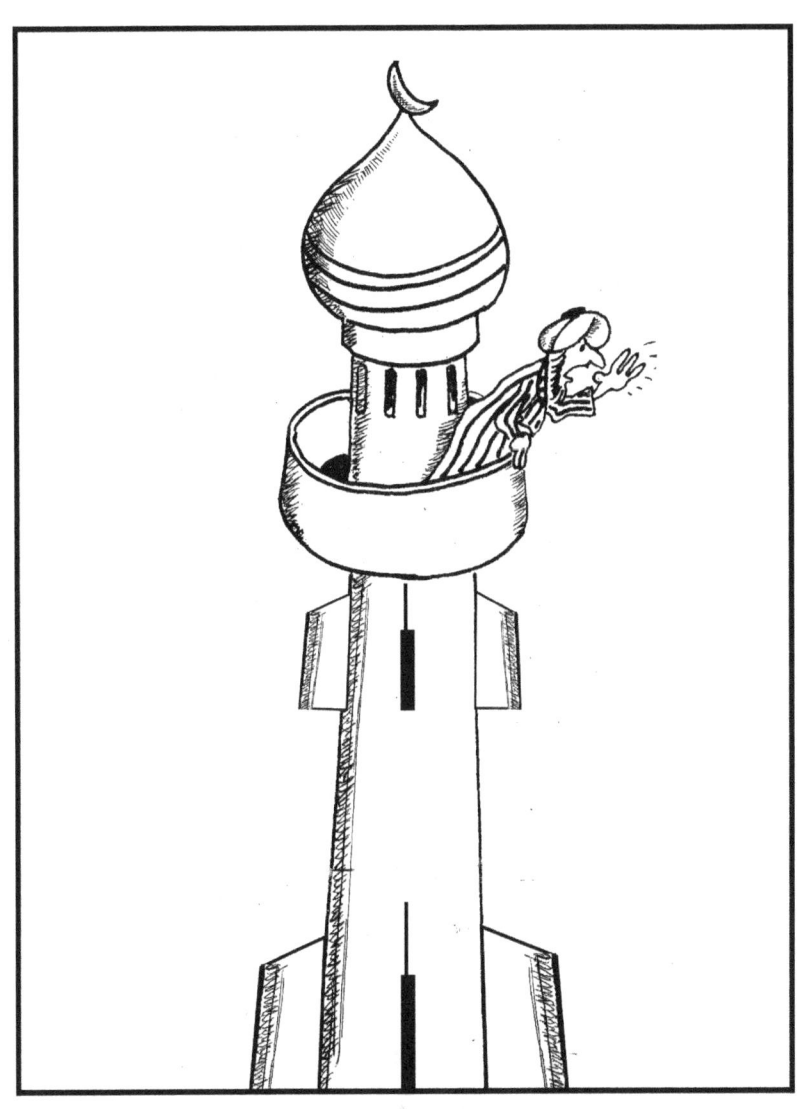

**Word of Allah can reach even the deaf but people of the world don't except evil breath.**

When you encounter the Karifs on the battlefield, cut off their heads until you have thoroughly defeated them and then take the prisoners and tie them up firmly.

*Quran Surah 47:4*

When ye meet the Unbelievers in fight, smite at their necks. At length, when ye have thoroughly subdued them, bind a bond firmly on them. Thereafter is the time for either generosity or ransom, until the war lays down its burdens. Thus are ye commended, but it had been Allah's Will, He could certainly have exacted retribution from them Himself, but he lets you fight in order to test you.

*Quran Surah 47:4*

Allah has promised those among you who believe and do righteous good deeds, that He will certainly grant them succession in the land, as He granted it to those before them.

*Quran Surah 24:55*

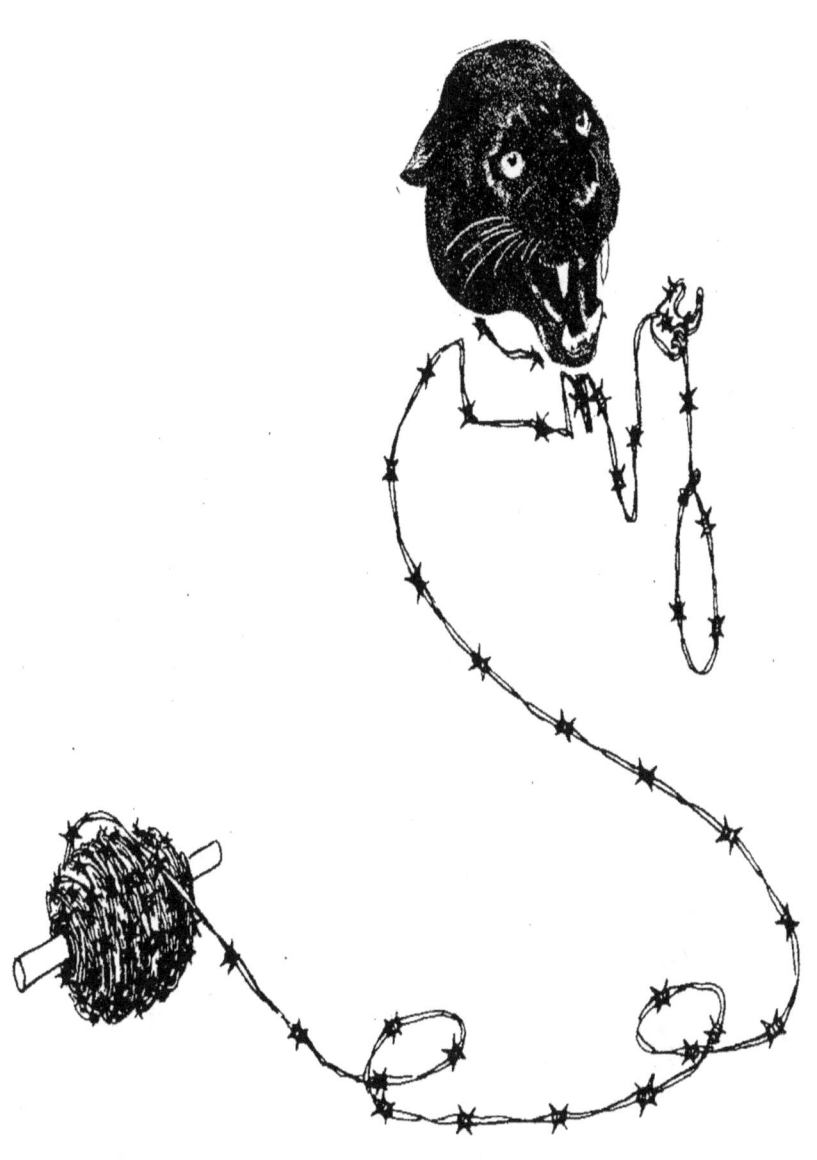

**A JIHADIST is more dangerous than a puma a JIHADIST is a half-human puma.**

Not equal are those observers who sit at home and receive no hurt, and those who strive and fight in the cause of Allah with their goods and their persons. Allah hath granted a grade higher to those who strive and fight with their goods and persons than to those who sit at home. Unto all in Faith hath Allah promised good. But those who strive and fight hath He distinguished above those who sit at home by a special reward.

*Quran Surah 4:95*

The person who participates in Holy battles in Allah's cause and nothing compels him to do so except belief in Allah and His Apostles, will be recompensed by Allah either with a reward, or booty if he survives or will be admitted to Paradise if he is killed in the battle as a martyr. So do not become weak, nor be sad, and you will be superior if you are indeed true believers.

*Quran Surah 3:139*

# A welcoming entrance to ISIS.

## As a matter of fact, it is an entrance into a trap.

# CONCLUSION

Many years ago the great French philosopher Voltaire said, "I will detest individual tyranny less than collective tyranny. A despot always has some good moments; a group of despots, never."

"Murderers are not monsters, they are men. And that's the most frightening thing about them."
*Ali- Sebold*

"Fanatics can justify practically any atrocity to themselves. The more untenable their position becomes, the harder they hold to it, and the worse the things they are willing to do to support it."
*Mercedes Lackey*

ISIS copied their barbaric behavior not only from MuhamMAD but from Hitler's playbook. Heinrich Himmler, chief of the Nazi Gestapo, said, "The best political weapon is the weapon of terror. Cruelty commands respect. Man may hate us but we don't ask for their love, only for their fear."

**ISIS - enemy of civilization deserves extermination.**

ISIS is very persistent, tirelessly repeating their propaganda. They follow the advice of Joseph Goebbels, Minister of Propaganda in Hitler's Nazi Germany. "If you tell a lie big enough and keep repeating it, people eventually come to believe it."

"All propaganda has to be popular and has to accommodate the comprehension of the least intelligent of those whom it seeks to reach... through clever and constant application of propaganda, people can be made to see Paradise itself; and also the other way around, to consider the most wretched way of life as Paradise."

*Adolf Hitler*

When we describe ISIS as a group of terrorists, it is absolutely false. ISIS is not a group. ISIS is not even an organization. ISIS is an extreme idea to build a victorious khaliphate empire of vampires. This is an army of islamofascist revolution which is weaponized with the ancient, rotten (but even today) very effective ideology of supremacism. This army has absolute dedication to every word of the command of Allah and his messenger MuhamMAD. Their main idea is not to live and prosper in their personal lives but to be a martyr and die for the glory of Allah and earn eternal life in Paradise.

ISIS **hand of cooperation detrimental to any nation.**

They are fervently propagating their ideas, which are a synthesis of orthodox faith and extreme ideology. And they are successfully using modern tools of communication like the internet to recruit new followers. Today 50,000 websites are sympathetic to the ISIS cause. Everyday ISIS is sending close to one million tweets on Twitter. Every day our self-serving media is glorifying the ISIS animals. Western media does not have many photos or video of ISIS, so they show the same "achievements" of the modern cannibals again and again. I continue to see on TV the same photograph of machine gun-waving hoodlums.

Many years ago, Margaret Thatcher warned that "democratic nations must find ways to deprive terrorists and hijackers of the oxygen of publicity on which they depend."

It is not very effective to fight an ideology only with bombs and rockets. We have to contradict the ISIS ideology of brutal domination over the entire world with our beliefs and values. It must be a no-compromise fight for liberty against ISIS spiritual slavery. We are not descendants of fearful people; we are unafraid, and free Americans.

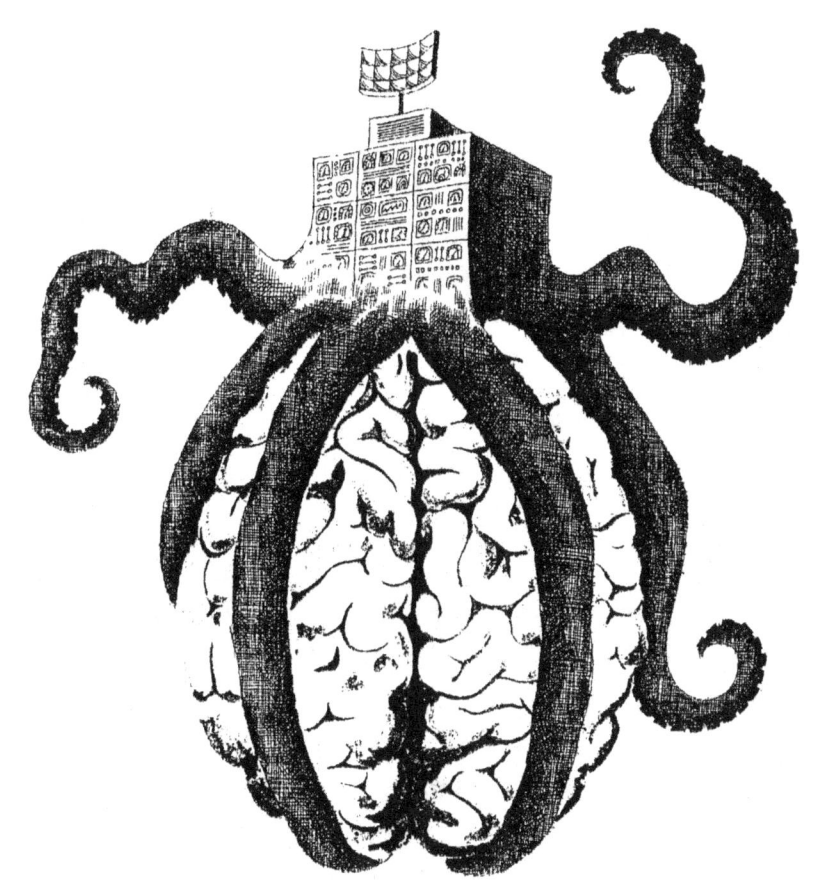

**Like cancer, which must be radically treated before it metastasizes, the roots of evil must be pulled out before they spring branches.**

We will not tolerate inhuman, uncivilized behavior from religious zealots. We have no other alternative but to stand tall and fight on all fronts: military, psychological, and ideological. We have to recognize that we are not a bunch of chickens led by a raven.

My cartoons are my ninjas. My aphorisms are my crusaders. I'm trying to attack, disgrace, degrade and diminish the evil of ISIS to the level of blood thirsty rats and ants.

Let us open an ideological front and show zombified youngsters that ISIS dinosaurs from Jurassic World are not superheroes in command of life and death, but are vile and depraved creatures.

Maybe youngsters, even with quite raw material in their heads, will be ashamed to join a society of primitive cockroaches. If we have no stomach to understand the danger of our situation with the help of our brains, later it will be more difficult to recognize it with the help of the other parts of our bodies.

Armageddon unholy universal jihad against our Judeo-Christian civilization has begun. If we hesitate even a moment to mobilize our resources in an anti-jihad; if we continue to trust our negligent, sick-with-political-correctness misleaders, the United States will fall into Apocalypse.

**That's our will: wherever a weed grows uproot it and kill.**

I hope Americans will rise
and stand tall for America.

The last one to laugh is the one
who is the first to shoot.

Let's protect the Second Amendment
of the Constitution,
to retain the right to shoot satirical barbs.

Optimists study English.
Pessimists study Chinese.
Realists study Spanish.
Anti-Islamists study our great history
and practice in the shooting range.

Sometimes an avalanche starts
from the falling of one stone,
but culminates in a major movement.

Let's start rolling.
"Extremism in defense of liberty is no vice"
because a terrorist is a bloody rat not a mice.
Therefore, "moderation in the pursuit
of justice is not a virtue."

**America is beautiful.
Don't let her turn pitiful.**

The inscription on King Solomon's ring said:
"This, too, shall pass."
But it will pass only
if we don't get tired of fighting.

As the old saying goes:
"For the devil to win, it is required only
that good people do nothing."

If we see a crime committed against humanity
and fail to raise our asses from the sofas
we become accomplices.

When our beautiful homeland is in the midst
of economic, political and military fires,
it is not the time for redecoration;
it is time for mobilization.

Time is running out. We live on a volcano,
and we must be prepared for a fight.

Talk peace but keep your ammunition ready.
"The price of liberty is, always has,
and always will be blood."

"The person who is not willing to die
for his liberty has already lost it
to the first scoundrel who is willing
to risk dying to violate that person's liberty.
Are you free?"

*Andrew Ford*

# It'll soon shake our windows and rattle our walls...

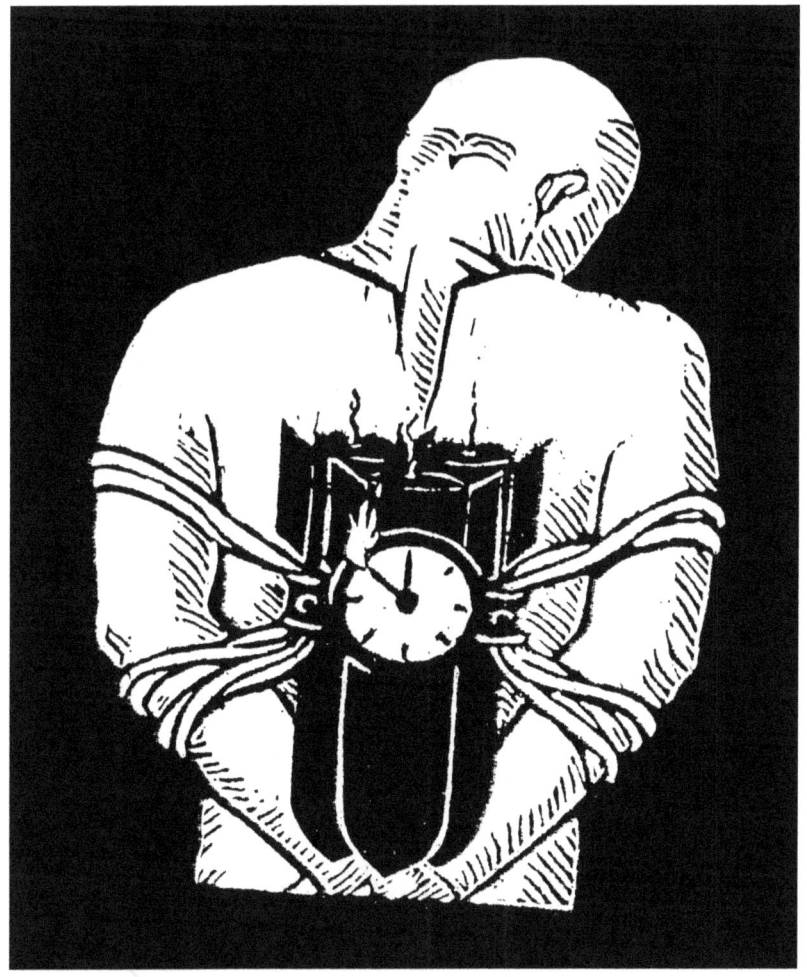

**because the government doesn't possess the balls.**

"Non-cooperation with evil is as much a duty
as cooperation with good."
*Gandhi*

"To stand in silence
when they should be protesting
makes cowards of men."
*Abraham Lincoln*

"Today, we need a nation of Minutemen,
citizens who are not only prepared to take arms
but citizens who regard
the preservation of freedom
as the basic purpose of their daily life
and who are willing to consciously work
and sacrifice for that freedom."
*John F. Kennedy*

"Let every nation know,
whether it wishes us well or ill,
that we shall pay any price,
bear any burden, meet any hardship,
support any friend, oppose any foe
to assure the survival and success of liberty."
*John F. Kennedy,
inaugural address, 1960*

"And just as the terrorist seeks
to divide humanity in hate,
so we have to unify it around an idea.
And that idea is liberty."
*Tony Blair*

So stand strong with the belt of truth
tied around your waist
and the protection of right living on your chest.
To do this you must always
be ready and never give up.
*Ephesians 6:10-18*

Today there is a direct question:
"Who will win?"
Either Islamist-cannibalist
ideologically crippled jihadists
or a free people.
So, gloves off America!
Time to stand firmly in defense of our values,
our civilization
and the future of our children.
"If not we, who else? If not now, then when?"
*Ilya Katz,
Satirist-General, Screw-sader against Islamofascism.*

**ISIS, time for mourning bell, America open the entrance to hell.**

**If we can't understand our situation with the help of brains, it will be too paintful to do it with the other parts of the body**

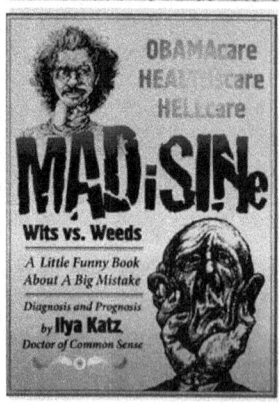

Please send your inquiries for books and ebooks to: IngramSpark and Amazon Create Space

*More information*

*www.katzforussenate2016.com*
*www.savemotherland.us*
*www.katzvsrats.us*

*katzconcern@gmail.com*

It is not recommended to look into the muzzle of a loaded gun, but try - get these books.

www.ingramcontent.com/pod-product-compliance
Lightning Source LLC
Chambersburg PA
CBHW070759100426
42742CB00012B/2196